THE WIZARD'S WAY
TO
POWERFUL
PRESENTATIONS

THE WIZARD'S WAY
TO
POWERFUL
PRESENTATIONS

Secrets from Wizards of the Past
Revealed for
the World Changers of Today

TOBIAS BECKWITH

Triple Muse
Publications

Printed by Createspace, an Amazon company. No part of this book may be used or reproduced in any manner whatsoever without written permission except in the case of brief quotations embodied in critical articles and reviews.

For information, visit www.wizardsway.net
E-mail: tobias@yourmagic.com

FIRST EDITION

Illustrations and cover design by Kiva Singh
www.kivasingh.com

Edited by Carolyn Uno (Tigris)
Book design and layout by Tobias Beckwith
www.tobiasbeckwith.com

Library of Congress Cataloging-in-Publication Data has been applied for.
ISBN 0-9779843-6-2

*Dedicated to Poppy, Yoshi, and
Scrapper.*

Contents

Chapter 4: Three Rules of Three — 57

Chapter 5: It's Always a Show — 65

Chapter 6: It's Always a Sale — 75

Chapter 7: Creating Transformational Experiences — 83

Introduction
Why Learn to Present Effectively?

Introduction: Why Learn to Present Effectively?

True world changers work largely by leveraging the efforts of others. One person can only do so much by himself. Through his influence over others, though, he can bring about profound change. Think of Mohandas Gandhi, a small man given to the simplest possible way of living. He had no mansion, no army, barely any clothes; his most prized possession was his spinning wheel, yet he managed to take back his native India from one of the greatest empires of all time, the British Raj. How did he do it? Quite simply, by influencing and inspiring others, both his own followers and those who then controlled the Raj. Or think of Steve Jobs, who managed to shift the direction of Apple when it was foundering, nearing bankruptcy; through his vision and ability to persuade others—both employees and customers—he turned the company around and made it one of the largest and most valuable in history. If you knew how these world changing real wizards managed their extraordinary feats, could you create the same level of change? Of course you could! That's what this book is about.

Powerful Presentations Help You Change the World

Who wants the power to cause change? If we're honest, I think we all do.

I know, I know. You've probably been taught to think of power as something ugly—something wielded by megalomaniacal despots, unfeeling governments, and profit-motivated corporations, something nice people should look at with disdain or perhaps with fear. Embracing that attitude, however, will ensure that you'll never actually have any real power. It's not an attitude you can afford if you're going to run a company, lead an organization, or make a real difference in this world.

When you consider it, don't we all want the power to change others so they will give us our own way? Okay, that's the selfish point of view, but don't we all want to create a better world for our family, to change the things we find unpleasant, unfair, or just inconvenient? And why don't we make the changes we want? Most of us feel helpless. What can one little person do to stem the tidal wave of events coming at her—or at least to steer those events in what she thinks is the right direction? What can even a small group of people do to shift the momentum of a lumbering bureaucracy, the long-entrenched dogma of a society, or the willful surge of a powerful industry?

The truth is that you can have that power. You can change yourself and the world around you, but in order to do so, you'll probably need to enlist the aid of others. In my previous book, *The Wizard's Way*, I set forth a program for would-be wizards—a collection of techniques they can use to change the world in lasting and meaningful ways. One of the most effective ways we can catalyze change is by leveraging the time, efforts, and money of other people. We gain this ability primarily by learning to present inspiring visions that persuade others to take the kind of massive action that is beyond any one of us. Leveraging the resources of other people is one of the best reasons to develop your ability to deliver powerful presentations.

What are some other reasons?

Poor Presentations Do Damage

We've all experienced the pain of bad presentations. Whether from fellow workers who drone on interminably with their reports during a meeting, salespeople whose inability to create rapport drives prospects away and fails to make sales, or top executives who waste time and money with ineffective speeches at large events the company has paid for, bad presentations cost valuable time, money, and even customers.

Waste Time and Money

When you call a meeting in your organization, you're burning valuable man-hours and woman-hours. If you have a meeting that ten people are required to attend, and that meeting goes on for 30 minutes, you've just paid for at least five person-hours of work, but probably more, given that people have to spend time getting to and from that meeting, preparing for it, and getting back into normal work mode when it's done. If communication during the meeting is muddled and confusing, the cost in time and money can be huge.

When we fail to communicate effectively, we leave others not knowing precisely what we want from them, so they waste time trying to guess or doing the wrong thing.

Waste Resources

Poor communication can waste more than time. Conferences go on for days longer than they need to, wasting time and money. Workers perform their tasks inefficiently, wasting material resources. What's more, miscommunication—when parties to a communication fail to understand one another—can lead to work being done wrong, to unnecessarily hurt feelings, or worse. In each of these instances, time, effort, and often physical resources must be expended to get back to a place where the parties can again work effectively together.

Make You Look Bad

I've been to dozens of large corporate functions hosted by Fortune 500 companies at which top executives giving talks to their thousands of employees or partner companies seemed unable to express their points clearly, unnecessarily complicated their messages, and generally bored all present. As a result, their company looked ineffectual, incompetent, and worse. Incompetent presentations send the message that you are either incompetent or just don't care.

Lose Audience Interest

Presentations that lack a clear purpose or are poorly constructed or badly delivered rapidly lose the interest of their audience. Students fail to learn. Employees are left not knowing what is expected of them or are demotivated. Potential clients fail to buy. Does any of this concern you as a leader?

So let's learn to become great presenters, wonderful speakers, and skilled listeners—and put an end to all that unpleasantness!

Persuasion Is How You Succeed

If your company creates a great product but fails to sell it, there's a problem with the way you are communicating about that product. All presentations are actually sales pitches, and the more your people learn the principles of persuasive presentation, the better they'll become at selling your products or services.

On a more basic level, though, persuasion is how you get things done within an organization or community. Sometimes the what your presentation is "selling" is a call to action for your employees or a new attitude you want your team to take. Sometimes you're just selling the audience on new information that will affect their lives. In every instance, though, you must persuade your audience to accept the change you are advocating. You'll be able to measure the success or failure of your talks by whether or not your audience is persuaded.

Build Momentum for Change

The longer it takes to persuade others to do the things you need them to do, the longer it will take to reach the goals you've set. Sometimes a failure to persuade one person means you have to find others whom you *can* persuade, and the more attempts you have to make, the more time you waste. If you succeed more times than you fail, you'll reach success sooner.

Make Sales

If you run a business, your sales process is what brings in the revenues. Failure to sell is death for most businesses. Few activities in our lives require clear, well-conceived communication more than the sales process.

If your team botches their presentations, whether they are one-on-one communications or presentations before groups, your business will suffer.

It's generally helpful, when creating a new presentation, to think of it as a sales talk. All successful presentations have some purpose, and if the speaker thinks of that purpose as the thing they must sell, it will help clarify the choices she needs to make when constructing the presentation.

Creating Presentations Forces Clear Thinking

Folk wisdom says that the best way to understand a subject is to teach it. Teaching will illuminate how much you thought you knew but really don't. Nothing will help you clarify your real ideas and feelings about a subject like having to teach it to others.

It's the same with speaking. When you have to clearly express information and ideas on a particular subject, you have to master your own understanding of that subject.

Mastering your subject is especially important when you find yourself pitching your business to investors, customers, or anyone else whose support you need. If you cannot present your mission and your business plan in a way that is both clear and inspiring, you'll have trouble enlisting the support of others. Not only that, but you'll probably also run into all kinds of problems operating that business because you don't have a firm enough understanding of just what the business is and what it will take to make it a success.

Presenting Builds Your Personal Power

Most people are frightened of having to stand up in front of an audience and speak. Jerry Seinfeld once said, "For the average person, if you have to be at a funeral, you would rather be in the casket than doing the eulogy!"

We grow by facing our fears, not by running from them. So putting yourself into situations in which you have to give talks will help you grow and build your personal power. You'll be surprised at how good it feels to overcome this anxiety. A bit later, you'll probably be even more surprised to discover how much fun it is to deliver talks that actually influence others to take action and help change the world.

Wizard Precepts for Presenters

Chapter 1: Wizard Precepts for Presenters

Wizards have a set of ideas, principles and techniques that allow them to do what others see as being impossible, and help them create change in the world. Here are just a few of those "secret techniques," that will give us a framework for creating better presentations.

Vision and Purpose Come First

Without a clear vision, no presentation can be completely effective. Defining what you want your talk to accomplish—what change it should create—is the first step to success. Most public speakers who fail do so because they have no idea of what it would mean to succeed.Fuzzy thinking at the beginning leads to confusion, boredom, and frustration down the road. Define your purpose, and most of the other work of creating a presentation will fall into place.

If you don't know where you're going,
you might not get there.

—Yogi Berra

Aiming for a Sale

One way of discovering your purpose for a particular talk is to think of every talk, every paper, every presentation in terms of making a sale. What are the specifics you want to change as a result of your talk? What actions should those who hear you take when you are finished? How will you get the audience to buy in to your message? I know I'm repeating an idea here, but it's important. We'll come back to this later.

Aiming for Transformation

Why present if not to create some change? Do you want your listeners to be happier, more loyal, more productive, more innovative? How will you persuade them to change? Figure that out, and you will be halfway to success.

Experience Creates Change

We learn best through experience. And learning—education—is a transformative process. Every experience we have will change us, so it's important to design the experience your presentation will provide so that you create the specific change you want to see.

The Speaker's Experience

As a speaker, you create your own experience and that of your audience. What sort of experience do you want to have? How can you make this particular talk into that kind of experience for yourself? Do you like to hear people laugh? Gasp? Applaud? Engage you in further discussion? You can make all that happen by creating and delivering a talk designed to do any or all of those things.

The Listeners' Experience

It pays to remember that your talk is creating an experience for your listeners. You are doing more than just conveying information, and the experience you provide will have a lot to do with how the information is received. Consider how you'll make people feel when you show and tell them the things you want to convey. Consider the stories you want to tell from the listener's point of view. What sort of direct experiences can you provide for them? Will this particular audience feel the same way you do about those stories?

Understanding the Process of Change

In addition to knowing how to define a clear purpose and construct a compelling presentation, you need to understand how change takes place for human beings and you need a toolbox of methods for creating change.

When we want to persuade, there are three areas we might influence: rationality, emotion, and resistance to change. These can be likened to a rider (rational mind), an elephant (emotions and the subconscious), and a path (resistance to change). Imagine an elephant walking on a path through a thick jungle with a rider on her back, and you'll have a good idea of the relative strength of the rational, conscious mind versus the subconscious emotions. You'll also understand the power of the available, easy path to influence the rational mind and the emotions.

The Rider

Most speakers make their appeal to the rider.

Clear logic is of great value when appealing to the logical mind. What are your (and your audience's) basic assumptions going in? Starting with those basic assumptions, and following with if-then logic to show them how and why the change you advocate is needed ought to work, right?

The Elephant

Research has shown that most decisions are made not by the logical, rational mind but by the subconscious, emotional mind. Ori and Rom Brafman wrote a whole book called *Sway: The Irresistible Pull of Irrational Behavior*, in which their whole point is just that: "It's easy to forget that under the surface we humans are still influenced by irrational psychological forces that can undermine a logical perspective on the world around us. The fact is, all of us are swayed at times by factors that have nothing to do with logic or reason."[1] That elephant is much larger than its rider!

---

1   Ori Brafman and Rom Brafman, *Sway: The Irresistible Pull of Irrational Behavior*, page 180

Although many people long for things to be different, most of us are emotionally attached to being just as we are. After all, we've spent our whole lives becoming just who we are and we're comfortable with that person. This attachment makes real change—the kind that begins with changing ourselves—something that we resist. We put up emotional blocks in the form of annoyance, anger, depression, and the like—anything to avoid moving out of our long-established comfort zones. The problem here is that your rider, the conscious mind that believes it wants to change, isn't always even aware of the desires of the elephant (the subconscious) to resist that change. If you really want to create change, then, it's extremely important that you get your (and your audience's) rider and elephant in alignment with one another.

> *Every body perseveres in its state of rest, or of uniform motion in a straight line, unless it is compelled to change that state by forces impressed thereon.*
>
> Isaac Newton, *Philosophiae Naturalis Principia Mathematica*

Sir Isaac Newton's first law of motion, the law of inertia, also applies to human affairs. We all tend to remain comfortably at rest or in the motions to which we are habituated, unless we are jolted out of those paths by sufficient force. How will you make sure your story generates sufficient force to jolt your audiences out of the paths to which they're accustomed, the paths that lie well within their comfort zone?

Stories are a means of giving us vicarious experience. When the heroine of a story has an experience, we mirror that experience—have a less intense version of it—within ourselves. We empathize with the heroine and experience her pain, triumph, disappointment, or joy. We think, "That poor person. I must be careful not to make the choices she made that led her to this unhappy state." We find ourselves wanting to make the changes in ourselves that will help us become more or less likely to share the fate of that heroine. And yet our joy or pain is less intense than if we actually had had the experience the character in the story has. We can get the lesson of that experience without paying as high a price.

By now, you should be starting to realize what a powerful tool stories can be for your presentations. They will often become your best way of guiding the audience's emotional state of mind, so that it aligns with the purpose you've set for your talk.

The Path

We are often controlled by the path we are already on, and the inertial comfort involved in staying on the path we know. Every day, I drive all the way around a small mountain to get to a cafe on the exact other side of the mountain. I actually go two or three times as far as the cafe is from my home if I were to fly directly to it. But there is no road, no path that follows that most direct route. My travel is governed by the path that's available. So it is with the elephant and rider. They will often find themselves acting on the basis of the path most easily available to them.

The concept of available paths offers the persuasive communicator an opportunity to catalyze change. If we, as powerful presenters, are able to show our audience a more efficient path or alter the paths available, we will often find it much easier to help audience members change their behaviors.

When encouraging a particular action or change, often the easiest way to convince others is by changing the paths available to them (or changing their perception of the paths available). Since we are already inclined, both rationally and emotionally, to take the path of least resistance, pointing out a small change that alters the available paths is often the best leverage point for creating real change.

Here's an example: My friend Hank recently moved into a new neighborhood. Along the most obvious route between his home and office, there was a Krispy Creme Donut shop. Hank and his wife both loved Krispy Creme donuts, and so he found himself stopping almost every day on his way home from work to pick up fresh donuts. Sometimes he even stopped on his way to work for a morning snack. Before long, Hank noticed he had put on ten pounds and added an inch to his waistline. "I'll just cut down my stops at the donut shop," he thought. But most days, he still found it difficult to make it past the shop without stopping.

Then one day, Hank invited a co-worker over for dinner. They both left the office parking lot together, but when Hank got home, the co-worker was already there. "How did you manage to get here before me? I was ahead of you on the way out of the parking lot."

"Yeah, but you seem to be taking the long way around. If you use the highway, you wind up going two miles out of your way. I took Wisteria Way, which, even though it's a surface street, comes almost directly here. And you avoid all the little strip malls and traffic lights between your place and the highway. It's almost 10 minutes faster."

The next day, Hank tried Wisteria Way, and sure enough, cut almost 10 minutes off his commute. He started using that route all the time. Not surprisingly, he started losing weight, too. The new route didn't go past the Krispy Creme shop, and so the temptation to stop every day was removed.

Emotional Appeals

As you can see from the metaphor of the elephant, rider, and path in the preceding section, your best bet for persuading an audience to take action or change their point of view will be an emotional appeal. Seduce that elephant! An emotional appeal can take many forms.

Positive and Negative Emotional Arguments

I'm sure you've noticed that, in many respects, people are different from one another. Some respond best to positive stimuli. "If you do this, look at what you'll get!" Many people are moved to action only by negative emotions. Threats work on them: "Do this, or else this horrible thing will happen." Or "How could you continue to let that terrible thing continue to happen, when it would be so easy for you to change it?"

Reciprocity

Reciprocity is the idea that if you give me something, I'll probably give you something in return. Reciprocity is an extremely powerful tool for persuading others to take action.

An example from Robert Cialdini's book *Influence* shows how the principle works. He describes a common strategy used by people who sell cars: They offer you a soda or a cup of coffee just as your meeting with them begins. As a result, you understand that they've given you something and you feel obligated to reciprocate. Unfortunately for you, the only thing you have to offer back is your agreement to terms you might have been unwilling to accept without further negotiation if you didn't feel obligated. Those cans of soda, worth less than a dollar each, often cost buyers thousands of dollars!

How can you use this technique in your presentations? To some extent, the reciprocity is built in. You are offering your hard-won knowledge and insights, your time and effort just to entertain the audience with your talk. They owe you their attention, their responsiveness. And if you're really good, they might feel they owe you real consideration of the ideas you present or the transformations you advocate.

You can also offer an audience a technique that can help them, teaching them by taking them through the technique—a simple movement, a chanted motto, or something else. As you finish teaching the technique, you might conclude by saying something like, "I hope you'll use this in good health. It's my little gift to all of you."

Of course, you can also actually give something away during your talk or at the end of it. Many magicians who work parties and other events make a point of giving away candies or small souvenirs. I'm sure you've encountered the giveaway as a sales technique. A letter comes to you in the mail, pitching contributions to your favorite charity, along with pre-printed return address labels or a pen or a nickel. You can't send it back, so you have to accept the gift, and you feel bad if you don't reciprocate. The 50-cent pen buys your $50 contribution.

Radical Responsibility = Power

Taking full responsibility is one of the most important principles used by wizards. Wizards don't just sit around and wait for others to create the change they feel is needed in the world. They take responsibility for making things happen, and this mind-set helps them build the power to actually create change. An attitude that you are responsible for everything that comes into your awareness can be especially useful when you're making presentations.

No Bad Audiences

I've spent most of my life working with performers who work in front of live audiences (as opposed to working in front of a camera, not as opposed to working before dead audiences). Occasionally, one of them will come offstage after a performance and complain about "that awful audience." I feel sorry for those performers, because in blaming the audience, they've given away their own power to create a great experience. As the person presenting at the front of the room, you are the one who is responsible for the experience of everyone in the room. If they aren't responding in the way you expect them to, don't blame them. Instead, try to meet them where they are and help them have the experience they think they've come for. That may or may not be the experience you had planned to give, but once you've really connected with that audience, there's a much stronger chance that you'll be able move them in the direction you want them to go.

No Bad Situations

Just as there are no bad audiences, there are no truly bad situations. There are, however, many different kinds of situations you might find yourself in as a speaker. You will often be presented with situations you did not expect. The audience might be larger or smaller than expected. Technical support might be vastly different than you hoped for. You might find yourself outdoors when you expected to be inside. None of these are inherently bad situations unless you choose to see them that way. If you blame the situation for your own failure, you have given away your power to create a positive experience for all involved.

One way you can avoid problematic situations is to be prepared for a wide variety of situations. Some speakers travel with their PowerPoint presentations on large printed pads as a backup. If the projector dies or fails to show up, they can still use all of their graphics. Others design their talks so they won't rely on slides or other visual aids. Some speakers who work smaller local markets pack a sound system in the trunk of their car in case the sound system provided at their speaking venue is insufficient.

My friend Jeff McBride defines mastery as a performer as "When everything that can possibly go wrong has gone wrong, and you've figured out how to deal with it."

Question Everything

Questioning the assumptions underlying existing ideas and beliefs is a sure way to creating new solutions. Viewing a situation from unusual perspectives can also help others see a situation in new ways.

When you're presenting, it will pay for you to question everything. "Everyone uses PowerPoint." Not necessarily. "You have to stand at the front of the room." No, you don't. Ask any middle school teacher. "I read a book about presenting, and they said I had to structure my talk in a particular way." Don't believe it. (Even though I'm going to do just that a bit later on.)

More important than your decisions about the nuts and bolts of giving your presentation might be your willingness to question commonly held assumptions of your audience. When you want things to change, you're often encouraging audience members to do things differently than they are used to doing them. Often their reasons for continuing to do things that way boil down to "We've always done it that way," even though their argument for continuing might not sound quite like that. But if you can show that the assumptions on which they base their thinking are either intrinsically wrong or don't necessarily support the conclusions that lead to their current ways of doing and being, you'll have a chance of convincing them to change. First, though, you need to be able to question those assumptions in your own mind.

These, then, are the basic precepts from the world of true wizards that will most help you in your quest to become a persuasive and effective communicator and a power presenter: vision, purpose, the ability to create transformative experiences for our audiences, an attitude of radical responsibility, and a willingness to question basic assumptions, both your own and those of your audiences. You'll learn more about how each of these principles applies in the chapters that follow.

Meta-skills for Presenters

Chapter 2: Meta-skills for Presenters

Wizards understand that certain skills underlie other, more specific skills. Knowing how to learn, developing your memory, understanding logic, knowing how to tell a story and how to use your voice and body as tools to help you communicate, and more—these are meta-skills that will serve you again and again. No matter the communications task, these skills will be in play.

Memory

We've all suffered through presentations in which the speaker reads his talk verbatim from his notes. Often such speakers never look up, lack vitality or inflection, and lose us within a minute or two of beginning their talk. Only slightly better is the speaker who uses her PowerPoint presentation instead of notes but still reads the whole talk from the PowerPoint slides. Neither of these speakers belongs on a stage giving a talk. They might be brilliant at what they do, but they totally fail at the process of connecting with and inspiring an audience through their presentation.

A slight improvement over either of the first two examples is the speaker who uses a teleprompter, projecting his or her complete talk on the screen. I've experienced some very good speakers who use a teleprompter and others who are obviously just reading what's on the screen before them. The good speakers have obviously been through the talk a number of times, understand what they want to say, and use the teleprompter just to help them stay on track. Most of their energy goes into actually getting the message across to their audience. They refer to their slides when appropriate but don't allow the slides to overpower their presentation. They engage their listeners, making eye contact and addressing different segments of the audience.

Speakers who rely heavily on their notes, in whatever form they access them, will fail as presenters.

Speakers need to develop memory techniques. Actors have many ways of learning lines. They have to, especially if they work in television, where they must learn the equivalent of a new one-act play every week.

The simplest technique for memorization is the brute-force method. You read and repeat sections of the talk again and again until they make their way into your muscle memory. A second method is to think of the script as a song. You don't actually sing it, but you become very aware of just how you inflect each sentence and the rhythms of the words. I'm sure you've noticed how much easier it is to learn the lyrics of a song than it is to memorize a chunk of prose of similar length. Melody, rhythm, and all the elements that go into making music help you associate the lyrics with other things in your mind, and that helps you learn faster.

Many speakers break their talk into manageable chunks. If you speak to different audiences about slightly different subjects, you might find that you have several such chunks that you can mix and match for different purposes. But how will you keep the running order straight in your mind? One method is to use a teleprompter, the slides in your presentation, or the ever-popular index cards or crib sheets carried with you or hidden about the stage, not to be read but to remind you which section comes next.

Even more effective, though, is the use of mnemonic techniques. Here are two, directly from *The Wizard's Way*.

Peg System

Many mnemonic systems use the fact that the more associations you have with a particular item, the easier it is to remember that item. In the peg system, we associate an item with another item already in our memory. This system is particularly useful for remembering things in a particular order—for example, the parts of a talk you will be presenting. You'll see why in a moment.

With the peg system, you first memorize a list of things you can use again and again. Here's an example of a list with ten pegs:

One = gun

Two = shoe

Three = tree

Four = door

Five = hive

Six = chicks

Seven = heaven

Eight = weight

Nine = wine

Ten = pen

The pegs rhyme with the number they represent because the rhyming provides an additional association that makes the peg easier to remember. It should only take you a few minutes to memorize your list of pegs.

The second step is to associate the list you want to remember with your pegs. Let's imagine I'm doing a talk about becoming a wizard power presenter, and these are the sections of the talk:

1. Why you want to do that
2. Developing your vision
3. Building your logic
4. Collecting data to support your argument
5. Building the sales aspect of the talk
6. Creating the show
7. Delivering the talk
8. Follow-up

Here's how to memorize that list, using the peg system:

1 = Gun = Why. Visualize a thug holding a gun up to your head and shouting "Why? Why? Tell me why, or I'll blow your brains out!"

2 = Shoe = Vision. Visualize a blue suede shoe with big eyes, and the eyes are looking everywhere. A shoe with vision.

3 = Tree = Logic. For some reason, the term logic tree just makes sense to me. I imagine something like an organization chart in tree form, and the tree and logic seem to go together.

4 = Door = Data. Imagine opening a closet door, and inside are stacks of plastic boxes filled with ones and zeros–data.

5 = Hive = Sale. Envision a beehive with a giant "For Sale" sign stuck in the ground in front of it.

6 = Chicks = Show. Imagine a little puppet theater with curtains opening on a brightly lit stage, and three baby chicks in a row doing kicks like the Rockettes–a show!

7 = Heaven = Delivery. Imagine going up to the pearly gates, and St. Peter holding up a sign that says "Stand and Deliver." Perhaps there's a UPS man standing there with a package to deliver to St. Peter.

8 = Weight = Follow-up. Imagine a mama duck with a string of ducklings *following* her. Each one carries a tiny barbell in its beak.

Okay, now it's your turn. What's first? The number one should make you think of a gun—and a thug holding it to your head asking you "Why?" Let's start the talk by telling the listeners why they want to learn to give great presentations.

The number two brings to mind a shoe with big googly eyes—a shoe with vision. It's time to talk about the importance of having a clear vision for the talks they'll give.

Three makes you think of a tree—a logic tree. That's right, you want to emphasize the importance of developing clear and compelling logic as a thread throughout their presentations.

Four is door, and you remember opening that door to find a closet filled with data. Now it's time to tell your audience how to collect and organize information and then select the strongest data to support their premises.

Five makes you think of that beehive with the For Sale sign. That's right; every presentation can be thought of as a sale.

Six reminds you of the chicks in the chorus line, putting on a show. Every presentation is also a show, and it's the listeners' job to make sure it's a good one!

Seven brings heaven to mind, with St. Peter and his sign: "Stand and Deliver." Oh, yes, and that delivery man. Time for some tips on delivering that talk in front of a real audience.

Eight. Let's see, eight means a weight. Ah yes, those little ducks following their mother, each carrying a barbell. What was that supposed to indicate? Oh, that's right, it's to remind you about follow-up—the actions you want the listeners to take as a follow-up after hearing this talk.

That's how the peg system works. You memorize one list, then create vivid visual associations with the things you want to remember and each of the pegs. Your brain will naturally do the rest!

The Memory Palace

In the memory palace, also known as the *loci* system, we associate the items we wish to remember with a place instead of a peg. Here's the theory: You already have a great many places that you know very well—your home, your office, rooms within each place, your route to work, places you like to visit, and so on. Magician and mentalist Derren Brown has stated that much of London has become a memory palace for him.

Here's an example of how the memory palace can work. Imagine I'm doing a talk on the key points you need to consider in building a business. Suppose those key points are summarized in the following list:

1. Mission / Purpose

2. Team

3. Strategy

4. Legal Considerations

5. Financial Systems

6. Communications

7. Marketing

8. Product Excellence

9. Leadership

The location I'll use for this list is the backyard and pool behind my old home in Las Vegas as I would experience it as I would go for my morning swim. As I go out the back door, there's a table in front of me, surrounded by five chairs. At the other end of the patio is an outdoor rocking chair and then, at the end of the pool, a white plastic lounge chair. Also near that end of the pool are the pool pump and filter; the pool jogs to one side, where there's a water slide you can use to slide into the deep end. An interesting mandala pattern is painted on the bottom of the pool where you land when you go down the slide.

It's time for the talk. I present my introduction, and now I want to talk about each of the items on my list. First, I imagine opening the door onto the patio; there, in the middle of the table, is a giant cake with the word *Mission!* written in frosting. A tiny showgirl pops out of the cake and shouts, "I'm your purpose. Pay attention to me!" Sitting around the table, dressed in bright orange rugby jerseys, is my team, the folks who have helped me build my business. As I look over at the rocking chair, I see someone has propped a whiteboard there and scribbled on it diagrams of plays the team might execute—our strategy. Moving on, I notice the lounge chair, and sitting in it, in his best $5,000 suit, is my lawyer, with his briefcase, holding out a contract for me to sign. That's the legal part of my business. Over on the filter unit behind my lawyer, there are piles of $100 bills, fresh from the bank, which will all become mine when I sign that contract. That's the financial part of the business. With all that taken care of, it's time to move to the water slide. I climb up the steps of the slide and signal my team to follow me, waving and whistling to get their attention; it's all about communication! I sit at the top of the slide and shout, "Watch me!" Laughing, I slide down into the deep end. As I land with a splash, I see the word *Marketplace* written on the bottom of the pool. Ah, yes. Pay attention to marketing. I swim to the other end of the pool and begin my laps for the morning. Time to make myself stronger, sharper, to build my personal—and product excellence. This is the payoff for having paid attention to everything else. Product excellence! As I finish my last lap, I climb out of the pool, and my team follows. They've all done great work and followed my example every step of the way. We're all inspired, and I feel that I've provided the leadership needed for this particular experience.

Your turn. Take yourself through my morning swim, and see how much of the list you remember. What do you see when you open the door? Who is sitting around the table? What do you see on the rocking chair? Who or what is in the lounge chair? What is atop that filter unit? What does climbing the ladder for the slide bring to mind? When you slide down into the pool, what do you see? What do you think of as you swim those laps? Or when you're finished and climb out of the pool?

The whole sequence is easy for me to remember, because I've been doing that morning swim for years. You'll pick a locale that *you* know just as well. Once you've assigned the items to put in each location as you move through the space, you'll be amazed at how easy it is to remember them.

That's the memory palace mnemonic system.

Logic

The ability to think things through clearly, to figure out how things work, to evaluate the truth of things other tell us, and to derive new insights from already known facts—these are what make the human mind special and have contributed most to our rise from savagery to culture. All of these things have something in common: logic.

It is essential that you have a firm grip on the logic behind the arguments you will use to get your point across to your audience. If your logic is questionable, your listeners (some of them, anyway) will know. Strong, clear logic can be extremely persuasive, especially when you are speaking to audiences, such as scientists or the investment community, who are used to working with numbers and mathematical logic professionally. It's essential that you master a few basic principles of rhetorical logic.

Aristotelian Syllogisms

Aristotle and the Greek philosophers created a system of logic based on what they termed a *syllogism*. In syllogistic logic, you use two premises to derive a conclusion. Here is an example:

> *First premise: All birds are animals.*
>
> *Second premise: A robin is a bird.*
>
> *Conclusion: A robin is an animal.*

Of course, premises can be stated in various ways. Instead of "All birds are animals," the premise might be "No birds are made of stone." Because premises can be stated in different ways, strict rules are used to determine a conclusion and whether a given conclusion is valid.

One rule is that the premises must have one term in common with each other; otherwise, the resulting conclusion is a non sequitur, not a statement of logic—for example, "All robins are birds. Red squirrels live in trees. Therefore . . . ?" Obviously, no logical conclusion can be drawn from those two premises.

As another example, the "common" term might sound the same but actually have different meanings in the two different premises. My junior high math teacher demonstrated this issue for me:

"I can prove to you, using clear logic, that a peanut butter sandwich is better than happiness."

"No way!"

"Sure, here's how it goes: Nothing is better than happiness, right?"

"Well . . . okay."

"And a peanut butter sandwich is better than nothing, isn't it?"

"Uh, I guess."

"So it follows that a peanut butter sandwich must be better than happiness!"

See what happened there? The colloquial "Nothing is better than" isn't stating that the thing "nothing" (aka zero, nada, zip) is better than happiness. It is stating that "There is nothing that is better than happiness." We've been tricked by a figure of speech into drawing a conclusion from two premises in which the two common terms sound the same, but aren't really. Logic can be tricky!

Entire books have been written to explain how Aristotelian logic works. For a quick and very clear overview, I refer you to this web page: http://www.wikihow.com/Understand-Syllogisms

Propositional Logic and Predicate Logic

Propositional logic deals with stringing together a number of arguments or propositions to create a large system of logical truth.

Predicate logic is a more comprehensive system of logic than syllogistic logic or propositional logic. It is the form of logic we most often use in our everyday conversations, because the rules of predicate logic are the rules of everyday language. Aristotelian logic, as comprehensive as it may be, requires that its premises be formed in a certain way and that there be a clear path from one reasoned conclusion to the next. Predicate logic is based in Aristotelian logic but covers a broader range of situations.

Modal logic deals with less definite kinds of statements. Instead of "All birds have feathers," a statement in modal logic might be "Some birds can fly" or "Sometimes birds are blue." When we introduce modal terms, applying logic to create sound arguments becomes more complicated.

Logical Fallacies

Our application of logic often goes wrong. What first appears to be logically true may be the result of a logical fallacy. One of the most common ways that our logic can be faulty is when one of the premises isn't true. "All baseball players chew tobacco" might be such a premise. When we add the premise "This man is a baseball player," logically, this man must chew tobacco. But perhaps it's not true that all baseball players chew tobacco, or perhaps the man isn't a baseball player. Because one or both premises aren't true, the logic has derived a falsehood. The fact that the logic is based on false premises doesn't necessarily mean that this man doesn't chew tobacco; it only means that we haven't used sound logic to prove that he does.

In the preceding example, another misapplication of logic would be to have the second premise be "This man chews tobacco" and to assume that therefore "This man is a baseball player." Why is this assumption incorrect? Well, "All baseball players chew tobacco" (if it were true) doesn't mean that only baseball players chew tobacco.

Logical misinterpretation can also result when a term used in both premises means different things in those two phrases. We saw that problem earlier, in the peanut butter sandwich and happiness example.

These examples illustrate a few logical fallacies among dozens of possibilities. It's important that you avoid logical fallacies, partly because they will cause you to make statements that aren't true and partly because if people in your audience catch you using a logical fallacy to make a point, they may dismiss the rest of your presentation, even if your ultimate point is valid.

It can be fun to learn about the many ways logic can be misapplied. Many instances are common enough that they have their own names and origin stories. Want to learn more?

https://yourlogicalfallacyis.com/

https://en.wikipedia.org/wiki/List_of_fallacies

http://www.logicalfallacies.info/

Storytelling

Stories are how our minds make sense of the vast array of sensory streams that we encounter from moment to moment. Stories turn streams of abstract data into objects and actions with names and then with meaning and emotional import. If you want to reach your audience, if you want your presentation to actually affect behavior and create change, you will use stories.

As Albert Einstein famously reported, "Knowledge is experience. Everything else is information." By using a story to get your data into your listeners' minds, you allow them to have an experience, albeit a vicarious one.

"But," I can hear you thinking, "the subject of my talk is all about the data. I'm reporting on the results of a lab test, and my audience is used to getting information this way. This isn't the kind of information I can turn into a story." Well, I've spent some time teaching research biologists to lift the level of their presentations, and I'm here to tell you that you can turn raw data into stories, and when you do, it will make a huge difference in the quality of your presentations. While your audience may understand and relate to the raw data, unless you can make the information meaningful to them, most of them won't remember or care about it. And to make your data points meaningful, you need to turn them into stories. It's not as difficult as you might be thinking, and we'll return to this idea later.

For now, let me just plant the seed that there are many possible ways to weave a story. You might relate the story of the struggle you went through to come to the conclusions your presentation will impart. Or you might tell the story of an innocent bystander and his struggles, which the solution you're about to present will put to an end. You might even create a story in using the abstract items you present as characters in the story. (Did you see the movie *Inside Out*, in which the main characters are the emotions of another character?) As you can see, you can find many ways to turn your data, your raw information, into a story.

Vocal Technique

When I was young, I aspired to be an actor. So I studied voice—singing, speaking, character voice, and more. My studies in vocal technique have served me well over the years, most of all when I'm called on to give a presentation. If you're going to spend time in front of audiences as a speaker, improving your vocal technique will serve you as well. Take a "voice for actors" class or even a singing class at a local college or performing arts school.

Think, for a moment, about talks you've heard. Which ones were most memorable? Which were the most painful to sit through? I'm guessing your choice for the latter might be one in which the speaker had an unpleasant voice or one that lacked inflection. Perhaps the speaker had a speech pattern that was repetitive and annoying. For example, some young people seem unable to, like, say anything without using the word *like* in the middle of their sentences. Some of us say "um" when we're thinking. Others tend to end every sentence with an upward inflection, as though it were a question. None of these vocal habits will endear you to an audience, and some may distract listeners to the point where they are unable to hear your message. A few weeks with a good speech teacher might save those speakers from the ignominy of torturing their listeners.

When we get to the last chapters of this book, which discuss execution and delivery of your talk, I'll give you some simple vocal warm-up techniques as well as a few exercises that will help you deliver your talk with more power, in a way that truly expresses your enthusiasm for your subject and inspires your audience to share that enthusiasm. For now, start paying attention to those who speak for a living. Next time you watch a stand-up comic, pay attention to the way she uses her voice. Listen to a good news commentator, and pay attention to his diction, inflections, and so on. See if you can imitate some of these examples. Start singing in the shower; singing is a great way to build the range and strength of your speaking voice. Projecting a strong, supple voice is a meta-skill that will help you in developing other important communication skills.

Hypnosis and Trance

Okay, I'm not going to advocate that you start your talks with "Your eyelids are growing heavier" or some other such garbage. The last thing you want to do is put your audience to sleep!

Nonetheless, it is important to realize that most of us spend more time in trance than we are aware of. When you watch a good show or film on TV or spend time on your computer, your consciousness moves into the world on the screen. Sometimes friends or family members might speak to you, and you don't even hear them; you're in a trance.

Other times, after driving to work or some other familiar place, you might realize that you don't remember most of the process that got you there. You were in a driving trance.

People who teach meditation and yoga have told me, "The problem with most people isn't getting them to go into trance. It's getting them to wake up."

I have news for you: When you stand before a group and give a talk, both you and the group take on roles, one playing "leader" and the others playing "audience members," and that situation is automatically trance-inducing. You can do things that will break that trance, or you can take advantage of it. People in trance tend to be more suggestible. When you make suggestions, framed in a certain way, they are more likely to take those suggestions uncritically than they would be otherwise. Trance states are powerful, and I hope you'll use them wisely. Later in this book, we'll examine ways of inducing, breaking, and using trance states.

Building Rapport

I'm sure you've heard the term rapport. Building rapport means developing a common understanding with someone or at least understanding how they feel about something. On a deeper level, having rapport is the feeling that we are somehow the same as someone else, that we share the same values and feelings. We tend to trust someone with whom we have rapport.

When you are a presenter, it's important that you develop rapport with your audience. Your listeners want to feel that, although you may be quite different from them in many respects, you have sympathy for them and a clear understanding of what is important to them. If you want to sway their thinking and their actions, it's important that you start by recognizing and empathizing with their beliefs and state of mind before your talk begins. It is important that they feel the kind of connection with you that will bring about this trust.

How does one go about creating rapport?

Eye Contact

At one time or another, you've probably tried to hold a conversation with someone who will not make eye contact with you. It's very difficult, because the lack of eye contact makes you feel as though the person isn't paying attention to the conversation and leaves you feeling disconnected. On the other hand, someone who makes too much eye contact, continually staring you in the eye, can be equally disconcerting. As a presenter, you're unlikely to commit this second sin of communication, but many of us find the act of making real eye contact with an audience to be difficult.

Here are some basic guidelines:

At the beginning of your presentation, take a few seconds to make eye contact with and to actually see as many people in your audience as you can. Smile at some individuals. Nod at others. Really make contact, and notice them making contact back. This process should take only a second or two, but it will establish that you are "taking the stage." Too many inexperienced speakers are so uncomfortable in front of an audience that they feel they must fill every moment with sound and keep things moving. In fact, moments of silent eye contact, both at the beginning of your presentation and after key points, will help you establish your authority as well as emphasize and drive home important aspects of your talk.

Once you begin speaking, don't make the mistake of letting your eyes continually sweep the audience. Also avoid the mistake of hiding from the audience by turning to your screen and reading what is there. Instead, pick an individual in one part of the audience and deliver a whole phrase or sentence directly to that individual. Then pick someone in a different part of the audience and deliver the next line directly to them. Continue in this way. Occasionally, when you come to the end of a short section, take a moment of silence to let your point sink in while you scan the faces in front of you. Try to see who is getting it, and if some are obviously not with you, those are the ones you want to engage with your eyes during the next segment.

As you develop your skill and comfort level with this technique, you'll be amazed at its ability to give you firm command of an audience's attention.

Mirroring

Another important way to develop *rapport* is through mirroring. As human beings, we're programmed to sense and mirror the moods and actions of others, giving us an instinctive empathetic understanding of what someone else might be feeling and going through. One of the reasons we enjoy going to plays and movies is that mirroring allows us to have experiences vicariously that might have serious consequences if we were to have them directly ourselves.

As a performer or speaker, you can take advantage of mirroring in two ways:

First, because an audience will mirror your physical and emotional presence, you can influence the atmosphere of any given room through the use of your own body language, energy, and vocal tone when you enter that space.

If you bounce onto a stage with a big smile on your face, clapping your hands and shouting encouragement, you'll instantly create a corresponding response in your audience. On the other hand, if you slouch and shuffle your way to the podium, looking glum, and then begin to intone your speech in a depressing monotone, you'll create exactly that mood in the room. You can consciously cause an audience to shift moods just by drastically shifting your own. The audience will mirror you, because that's what they are programmed to do.

Second, you can establish rapport with people in an audience by first mirroring them. If they are somber and quiet, you can be somber and quiet until you feel they are with you. Next, you can help them shift their mood by shifting yours. If you're doing a presentation for just one or two people in a meeting, you can consciously mirror their postures and speech patterns until you see and feel the rapport kicking in.

Tuning In

One of the most difficult things for beginning actors to learn is how to actually listen to the other characters in their story. A common complaint of acting teachers goes something like this: "If your scene partner were to have a heart attack and fall on the floor, you would just keep going until the end of your line!" This kind of listening involves more than just your ears. I'm talking about tuning in to those you are speaking to in order to sense just how they are responding to what you're saying and doing. When you really connect in this way, you gain the power of a two-way interaction, even if you're the one doing all the talking. This connection can make the difference between your audience really getting the points you're trying to get across to them, or not. The feedback you get from paying close attention to your audience might also prompt you to elaborate on certain points more than you had intended, in order to make sure the points are getting through. If you're not paying close attention, getting as much feedback from the audience as you can, you'll miss out on many opportunities to succeed with your presentation.

Magicians who perform mental magic have to become masters at reading an audience. They'll be pretending to read someone's mind, perhaps saying something like "I get the sense of an older . . . man . . . no, it's a woman, isn't it?" As the magician says "older . . . man," he is watching the audience member's face closely. In this case, the face clearly indicates either "no" or "confusion," which means the guess was wrong, so the mentalist changes it before the audience member can say anything. As a result, the magician gets credit for a hit, just because he was able to correct himself before the audience member did. If you learn to read your audiences as thoroughly as mentalists do (and it only takes practice to do so), you'll soon find that your audiences are more and more enthusiastic about your presentations. Tuning in is another meta-skill that will serve you when you're involved in any kind of communication, not just when you're making a presentation.

Expressive Vocal Delivery

I'm sure you've had the experience of nearly dozing off during someone else's talk. Often, they are speaking about something that actually does interest you, but you just can't seem to keep your eyes open. It's embarrassing, but it's probably not your own fault.

If a speaker repeats the same intonation pattern over and over again, without much variation, it will often put audience members to sleep. If they don't go to sleep, many will wish they could, because even the most exciting material, when presented in a singsong, repetitive tone and rhythm, induces boredom.

When you're engaged in a lively conversation with friends on a topic that interests you, your speech is varied, reflecting your feelings about each item you're discussing. If something amazes you, you will sound amazed. Disgusted? It will show in your voice's rhythm, pitch, and inflection. When you speak before a group of strangers, though, you might find yourself more inhibited in your expression. And if you're feeling terrified just to be in front of a group, you might fail to make eye contact or to put any emotion or passion into your vocal delivery.

You can make sure this doesn't happen. When you rehearse your talk, don't rehearse by reading it word for word. Think about a whole sentence you're about to say before you actually speak it. When you rehearse, try going way overboard in the expressivity department. If something is sad, go overboard in making it sound sad. Shed a few tears. If it's happy, show just how happy you can possibly be! If it's funny, you might find yourself rolling on the ground as a result of your own joke. If you're angry, you might be screaming your guts out. At this stage, you want to take your expression way beyond what you will actually show to an audience. By rehearsing in this super-exaggerated way, you'll teach your muscles, your voice, and your emotional self to make the talk just a bit bigger than life when you present it before an audience. Your audience will thank you for the effort.

When I work with magicians to help them step up the showmanship for a given performance piece, I'll often ask them to run through the whole piece several times, each time in a different mode. One time, they'll sing the whole piece as though it were grand opera and they were in a hall designed to seat 5,000 people. The next time, they are to whisper the whole piece, as though telling it as a secret to one or two close friends. Then they are to shout the whole thing, like an angry coach in the locker room at halftime when his team has been underperforming. You get the idea; do your whole talk in each of these ways or other ways you come up with yourself, and you'll find it much easier to use those more extreme forms of delivery when you actually get before an audience.

Involvement

My friend Jeff McBride is probably the number one teacher of magic to magicians alive today. Here's a bit of advice he shares regularly: "When I perform, I'm not really interested in spectators. They are only there to spectate—that is, to watch, passively. I'm also not that interested in audiences, who are there to listen passively. No, I want participants." When you can move your audience from mere spectating and listening to real participation in your talks, you'll be taking a giant step to more effective presentation.

But how? It's actually quite easy. You simply give them things to do. "Repeat after me . . . " is a good beginning. "Give me a show of hands . . . " is another. Getting an audience to clap or chant with you can both lift the energy in the room and help you establish a "we're all doing this together" feeling of rapport. Remember to find as many ways as possible to elicit real participation from your listeners. The more you get them to move and speak during the presentation, the more they'll remember and the better they'll respond.

Developing these meta-skills—and I've really only scratched the surface in this department—is something that will help you immensely, not only when you make formal presentations, but in all of your different kinds of communication. Whether you are speaking, writing, having a conversation or engaging in some other kind of communication, you'll find these skills will enhance your overall capability in many ways. Memory skills, a command of clear logic, the ability to tell a good story, a more effective speaking voice, the ability to command a group using the trance states they automatically adopt, the ability to build rapport with a single person or a group—if you develop all of these, you'll find yourself rapidly becoming a more competent agent of change and more of a master of yourself and the world around you.

The good news is that you've begun. And there's more good news. Developing these meta-skills is a lifelong pursuit. You can always get better at any of them, and as you get better, they will help you master other, more specific skills as you need them.

Assembling the Ingredients

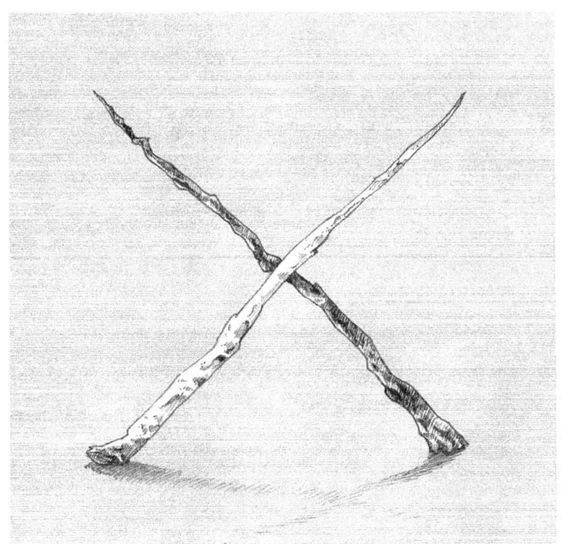

Chapter 3: Assembling the Ingredients

If your purpose is to change people, it helps to know their state of mind before you begin. You might think of your presentation as a wizard's spell or magical potion, designed to transform an audience from one thing into another. The spell for turning frogs into princes might do something entirely unexpected if applied to a fish, though. Once you know where you are beginning, you can start to construct the experiences that will move this particular audience to where you want them to be at the end.

Analyze Your Audience

Every audience—and every person you meet—is different from all others. What are the demographics of this audience? What are their mind-set, their mood, their beliefs in regard to your subject matter? You can guess at these things, or you might be able to interview one or two members of any given audience before you actually construct your talk for them.

Mind-Set

What is your audience's mind-set in relation to your purpose? Will you be preaching to the choir, meaning that you only need to reinforce views that people in the audience already embrace and perhaps inspire the group to action? Or are you there to open new avenues of thought and attitude—to truly transform the crowd? You need to know where the audience's attitudes and beliefs are before you set out to change them. It will also help you if you can assess their mood and general energy level. An audience of 3,000 at 7:00 in the morning will be very different from an audience of 30 at a lunchtime talk.

Prior Knowledge

What does your audience already know? Assuming that your audience knows more about your subject than they actually do is a sure way to confuse and bore that audience. What basic knowledge do they need before they can absorb the new material you have to impart? If they aren't already there, you need to start your talk by getting them up to that basic level so that they can understand what you have for them.

On the other hand, if this audience has a common set of metaphors or ideas they are used to accepting, you may be able to use these as a shortcut to your ultimate goal. Assumptions you don't need to prove, linked with clear logic to your desired outcome, can make it much easier to reach the goals you've set. Using those commonly held assumptions in this way is a form of leverage—something all real-life wizards use whenever they can.

Entrenched Positions

Does this group have deeply held beliefs about the topics you'll be speaking about? Are those beliefs in accordance with your message or at odds with it? How can you adjust the experience you provide in order to avoid or to make maximum use of the audience's emotional triggers concerning what you have to tell them?

Know Your Material

Collect all the materials that support your purpose. Every talk will have a different purpose and therefore will require different materials. Materials can take the form of graphics, objects that will aid your demonstration, arguments and logic supporting your point, or data that supports a business or scientific proposition, among others.

For example, let's imagine that your talk is a pitch to secure funding for your new business. You will want to have all the materials in place to convince those you are pitching that they will be making a sound investment. Your materials may include your current corporate balance sheet or projections on the size of your potential market, how fast you can grow, whether or not you already have a viable product, what your competition will look like, and so on. While you won't present all the details of this information in your short pitch, you will need to present the most salient and persuasive parts of it. If the story of how you came up with the product is interesting, you'll want to have a version of that ready. If you haven't already done the research and put in the thought to fully support your financial and other market projections, doing that will be part of your preparation for the presentation.

A good analogy to creating a great pitch is preparing a court case. One guideline for litigators is to never ask a witness a question that you don't know the answer to. The litigator must know all the answers because it's the litigator's job, just as it is yours, to lead her audience (a judge or jury) through the logic that will bring them to the desired conclusion. Any variation from the carefully prepared path may cause the case to go off the tracks. Gathering materials for your talk is the beginning of your preparation. As a general rule, if you want your talk to be a great one, collect at least three or four times the amount of supporting material that you expect to be able to use.

Create Your Argument

If you had to use only logic and cold, hard facts to create the change you want with your talk, what would you say? Remember our discussion on logic in the last chapter? Now is the time to put your logical abilities to work. What are the premises of your argument? Basic assumptions that your audience already agrees with will form most of these premises. If those you'll be speaking to don't already agree with the basic premises of your logical argument, there's very little chance they'll agree with your conclusions. Other options may be available to you, however.

Take the ongoing fight over global warming and what needs to be done about it. Those who accept the premise that the world is warming up and that it's at least partly due to human activities, including the release of excessive greenhouse gases, will be open to suggestions of steps we, as humans, need to take in order to reverse the trend. However, many people do not accept those basic premises; therefore, no argument can persuade them that we need to change our ways. Still, one might be able to get them to agree to the premise that average global temperatures over the past 50 years have, indeed, risen. Whether or not that is due to the activities of our society, it would still be good to adopt practices that might help to slow the temperature rise or reverse it. By choosing not to use the premise that we're causing the warming, one might still have a chance of convincing that part of the audience to change. A presenter who wants to move those people to accept arguments for change needs to either choose a different set of premises that the non-believers in the first set of premises will believe or go back a step or two and find premises that those people do believe that can lead them, through logic, to accept the premises they don't now believe. A clever thinker can almost always find more than one set of reasons why someone else might agree to a particular change. It's your job to find the right set of reasons for your particular audience.

Once you have your premises, it's time to use those premises to structure the logic that will lead your audience members to the conclusion you want them to reach. Your argument will take a form similar to this: "If you accept that A is true, and A implies B, then you must accept that B is true. If C is true, and C implies D, then you have to agree that D is true. Now we know that B and D are valid ideas. And we understand that if B and D are both true, that implies that E will be true (or necessary, desirable, whatever). Therefore, we should all embrace E and act accordingly." Your exact structure will vary, but you get the idea; your logic proves your point that the change you advocate is desirable and based on true thinking.

Note that you will not necessarily take your audience through the logic in this kind of bare-bones fashion. Certain parts of the logic string may be so self-evident that there's no need to spell them out. Other parts will be better accepted if they are illustrated through stories, graphics, or other means of persuading through emotion.

Collect the Sizzle

At this point, you know your purpose, your audience, your basic material, and the purely logical argument as to why the audience should come along with you to achieve that purpose. You have the skeleton of the information you need, but none of the meat. Now it's time to find the meat, put it on the grill, and make it sizzle!

A logical argument might be fine in a physics or law class. But logic doesn't address emotions. It doesn't make crowds stand up and cheer. It doesn't, by itself, create new movements or new cultures; it doesn't change the world. Wizards and presenters want to change the world, in both large and small ways. You want to change the world, and you understand that becoming a great presenter is one of the ways you can do that, or you wouldn't have read this far. So you need to get to people where they really make their decisions: their emotions. Still, you need the logic first.

Facts and Figures

Once you have a clear line of reasoning, it's time to collect the materials that will back up your case. Are there studies that prove either your premises or your conclusions? Find them, and collect both their data and the stories associated with them. If there is numerical data in the form of charts, tables, or the like, collect those, too.

Is there history that will help explain your presentation? Collect as many sources as you can—firsthand reports and authoritative commentary in news items, history books, or biographies. Have famous people commented on subjects that are related to your arguments? Gather their quotes. People tend to give more credence to points made by those they perceive to be authorities, so quoting authoritative sources can help you win your points.

Finally, consider what statistics might exist on your subject and to what extent they might be helpful in getting your message through. Collect statistics from trustworthy studies and sources. For example, the U.S.

Census Bureau might be a good source of the statistics you need. Fox News might not be. Your five-year-old quoting what he heard on the playground is most certainly not a reliable source for statistics.

In collecting the factual materials you need to support your case, again, the general rule is to collect as much as you can and far more than you're likely to include. It's also important to note that if there is factual material that might seem to work against your cause, you should collect and familiarize yourself with that, too. It's as important to know and address the obvious negatives as it is to get the positive reasoning across. Otherwise, your audience may feel you're trying to put something over on them.

Stories

Here's where creating a powerful presentation begins to require more of your creativity. We all make sense of the world by telling ourselves stories about what happens in it. We use our intellect and our ability to recognize patterns in order to take a string of events and turn it into something meaningful. That's how we make both meaning and memories. Occurrences that haven't been converted by our minds into a story are quickly forgotten and seldom make a deep impression on us. Thus, if you want to make an impression, you need to find ways to convert the straight facts supporting your arguments into stories—the more interesting and emotionally evocative, the better.

I've spent a fair amount of time directing magicians, helping them turn their magic tricks into entertaining shows. While an audience might be mildly interested when you show them that you can predict the card they will choose, given a seemingly fair process of selection from a random spread of cards, that's often not enough. That same audience will be exponentially more interested when that process is accompanied by a good story with strong characters, interesting plot twists, and an emotional climax.

My friend Robert E. Neale creates an effect he calls "Sole Survivor," which demonstrates the efficacy of a good story. The bare facts are that about a dozen cards are spread face down, randomly around the tabletop. The magician suggests that the cards represent the residents of a small village and that a plague is approaching the village. "Touch any two cards," he tells a spectator. "I'll decide which is to die." He does so, and turns the card face up. "Ah, the small boy, son of the doctor. What a shame. Now I'll touch two cards, and you decide which one dies." This is done, and the card turned up. "The wife of the physician. He must be distraught, and yet he must go on. . . . " The process continues, and each time a single card is chosen, the magician speaks of it as though it were a real person and he is reporting the news of the day. Finally, only one card is left. When it is turned up, it is the Ace of Spades. "The grave digger. How appropriate."

And so a simple trick—raw data—becomes a chilling story, something that is both moving and difficult to forget, once you've experienced it. With a bit of creativity, you too can find stories to illustrate your presentations—stories of what happened when people failed to make the changes you're advocating or what happened when they did. You might tell the story of how a particular conclusion was reached. ("We thought the answer might be X, but after experimenting, we found we were wrong. So we thought it must be Y, but that proved to be wrong, too. We were on the verge of tearing our hair out! It was almost by accident that we tested hypothesis Z, which seemed improbable. Here's how it happened. . . .")

Spectacle: Attending to the Visual

Okay, I'll admit that I do love a good Las Vegas show. Give me acrobats, showgirls, feathers, rhinestones, and sparkling lights any time! I lived in Vegas for a decade and helped produce and promote several such shows, so I know the power of spectacle—even when it's mostly empty spectacle—to hold an audience's interest. When the spectacle serves as dressing for solid content, it can be even more powerful. True wizards know that different people are moved through different senses; some of us are oriented more to sound and are moved by words and music, others are more visually or kinesthetically oriented. So providing a visual element to your presentations is important if you're going to reach everyone. But there's a right way and a wrong way to do spectacle.

Death by PowerPoint

You may have heard the expression "death by PowerPoint," which is popular largely because most speakers use PowerPoint (or Keynote or other presentation programs) so badly. A slide deck is the most common visual aid used by speakers today, largely because it is so easy to use and because it can provide the presenter with a false sense of security. When speakers suddenly lose their place (usually because they're under-rehearsed), they can simply look at the screen and know where they are in the talk. Too many speakers think it's a good idea to read their talk from their slides, which is a big waste of everyone's time.

Slides can, however, be a great aid. If you saw Al Gore's talk "An Inconvenient Truth," you've seen how a well-chosen graphic can make a point with far greater impact than simple words ever could. You can view the clip here: *https://www.youtube.com/watch?v=9tkDK2mZlOo.*

You can get a slightly different take on what makes a great slide deck by checking out any of the product launch keynotes given by Steve Jobs. Here's a link to a great mash-up of Jobs's talks throughout the years *https://www.youtube.com/watch?v=dkDMvYCvqyA,* but a quick on-line search will connect you with many more. Notice that in these videos, bullet points—the default for most PowerPoint templates—are used minimally, if at all. Complicated graphs and charts have been simplified down to the most basic information necessary to make the speaker's point. If you want to support your talk with complex charts and research graphics, it's better to include those in handouts that you distribute when the talk is done. Otherwise, they will distract your audience's attention from what you are saying while you're saying it.

Speaking of distractions, it's important to remember that your audience can focus on only one thing at a time, so make sure you know where you want them to focus. Do you want them looking at the slide or at you? Do you want them to read what is on a slide or to listen to the words you are speaking? If you want their attention in one place, make sure you're not supplying stimuli that will draw their attention elsewhere! Placing the audience's attention is something I work on extensively when I'm coaching a presenter, because it can make such a large difference in the way a talk is received.

Flipcharts and White Boards

You won't always have the luxury of using a computer and video system to support your talks. We've all experienced talks (while sitting in classes, for example), where the only visual aids available were chalkboards or whiteboards. Sometimes, even if you're expecting to have a screen and projector available, it's a good idea to also have your slide deck in the form of a flipchart: a large paper tablet with all of the slides reproduced so that you can flip through them just as if there were, indeed, a big screen.

With any form of visual support, the rules we discussed for using a slide deck continue to hold. Keep images and charts as simple as they can possibly be in order to reinforce the points your making. Make sure the visuals aren't there distracting from what you're saying when you need the attention to be on you. Plan things out so that, at every moment of the talk, you control where the audience's focus will be.

Props as Visual Support

If you've been to a magic show, you've experienced the power of using props. I've seen comedy jugglers who also create powerful metaphors with their juggling tricks. Physical objects used to help make a point can often be even more powerful than a visual on a big screen. With props, you have something that you can relate to, almost as if they are a second character on stage—which can be extremely useful if you're telling a dramatic story. Usually, the prop is smaller than you are, which makes controlling the attention given to the prop easy. Sometimes, you can actually use the prop to elicit more audience involvement. A beach ball can be tossed into the audience or you can invite audience members onto the stage to hold the ends of a rope or to help you handle another prop. People tend to support the things they help create, and by recruiting audience members to help you create an experience during your presentation, you'll be more likely to get their support.

I've been enjoying using magic tricks as metaphors to help audiences get involved with the message of the talks I've been giving, and adds a lot of fun to a talk. Audience members become characters in the stories I'm telling. The moments of astonishment give them an opportunity to applaud.

Provide an Experience

By far the most compelling and memorable thing you can do to move an audience is to provide them with an actual experience. Involve them. Make them actually participate by giving them something to do. An audience that is busy trying to figure out a puzzle you give them, coming up with an answer to a question you've posed, chanting a slogan, clapping their hands or that is otherwise physically or mentally involved is an audience that is experiencing your influence maximally. Of course, you have to choose the right experience to bring about the change you're after, so this is another part of your presentation that will require your creativity.

How will you find the right experiences to include? Think of what experiences you have had that caused you to feel strongly about the subject of your talk. Can you provide any of those experiences to your audience within the context of your talk? If not, perhaps you can think of a similar experience that you can provide. Perhaps you can provide a similar experience by asking the audience to imagine having the experience or by telling a story about someone having that experience.

Think about what emotions you want the experience you provide to inspire. What thoughts do you want to evoke? What physical sensations do you want the audience to feel? How many of the audience's senses can you engage with the experiences you provide? The more senses you can involve, the easier it will be for more of your audience to take in the new information , and more deeply they will feel and remember the experiences and therefore the points you are using the experiences to convey.

At this point, I've laid out the basics. You've learned the importance of defining your purpose for a talk, the power in seeing every presentation as an experience you create, and the necessity that you take full responsibility for that experience. I hope you've seen the importance of developing your own wizardly meta-skills, including memory, logic, storytelling, vocal technique and building rapport, and in becoming a truly competent communicator. In this chapter, you've learned the basics of assessing your audience, gathering your materials, and planning the strategy for moving a particular audience from where they are to where you want them to be. You've also learned a bit about the importance of giving you presentations that special sizzle that will make them both memorable and fun.

Fun is important. Oddly, it's especially so when we're dealing with serious topics. Keeping your listeners' minds open to new ideas, willing to change in the ways you want them to, is much easier if you can make sure they're having fun. The first step toward that end is to make sure you're having fun as you create and deliver your presentations. The following few chapters will help you look at this process of building a more effective presentation from several different points of view (another wizard principle), and I hope they will help to empower you and provide a sense of fun as you move forward.

Three Rules of Three

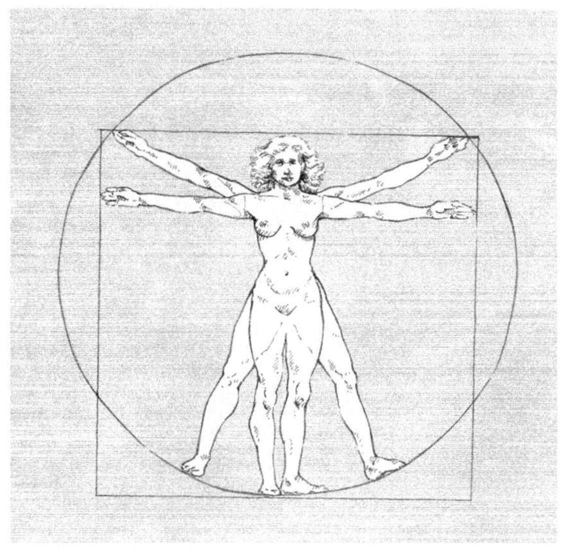

Chapter 4: Three Rules of Three

For some reason, our minds and memories are set up to group things into groups of three or four. Consider the music we listen to most: Waltzes are divided into three beats per measure, and a large portion of all other music has four beats per measure. Our minds seem to be set up to deal with clusters of three— and sometimes four. So here are my three rules of three.

Three Things at a Time

Since Aristotle wrote his *Rhetoric,* it has been known that most people will remember just three main points for any talk they hear. It will therefore pay you to organize your presentation into three main parts.

A first step, then, is to decide how you will define each of the three parts you want a particular audience to remember. Can you distill your talk into just three easily remembered phrases? This doesn't mean you won't take time to go deeply into each of the main three points or convince the audience they are important. It does mean getting clear enough in your own mind that you can state the three main premises clearly and succinctly. You will use those three main ideas to set up the main body of the talk and again at the end to remind the audience of what they've just heard. That way, you give them three memory pegs that will help them access and understand what the presentation was all about.

My personal preference—I like to divide each of my three main ideas into three smaller, supporting ideas. If I can't reduce a particular section to three, I allow for up to four, but no more. So a full presentation is unlikely to have more than three groups with three parts each. It's a good discipline to try to reduce a presentation down to that level of simplicity, if you want it to be remembered. For a presentation to be effective, it must be remembered.

This brings us to another kind of rule of three.

Beginning, Middle and End

A common way to structure a presentation is to create a clear beginning, middle, and end. Each of these three sections has a particular purpose.

Beginning

A good beginning does several things. First, it moves the audience into the world of your talk. "Once upon a time" takes us into a fairy tale world, for example. The beginning also sets expectations for the rest of the presentation. My friend, the mind reader Max Maven, says that a good opening should let the audience know "who you are, what you're going to do, and why they should care."

The "who you are" is important because, if you aren't already well known to a particular audience, this is what gives you authority. Sometimes an introduction read by someone else will be enough to establish your credibility, and sometimes you can weave a bit of who you are and why you're qualified to give this presentation into your opening story.

On the flipside, please don't spend your whole talk telling the audience who you are. Going on and on about yourself is self indulgent and boring, unless you are the subject of the talk and the audience has come just to hear about you. It's usually better to keep this portion short and to the point.

"What you're going to do" is important. If you can let the audience in on what they are about to experience, set the tone, and promise them fun along the way, it will spark their curiosity and prime your audience to better retain your major points.

Another consideration here is one we've mentioned before: What is the starting point for this audience? If you don't know where they are now, it will be tough to plan a route that will get them to where you want them. Set the stage by giving your audience the basic information, laying the groundwork they will need to accept your arguments and respond to your call to action.

Finally, why should they care? What, in this particular presentation, does this particular audience already care about? If they don't already care about your main points, how can you use the talk to link those points to things you know this group does already care about? Sometimes presenters go wrong specifically because they think an audience will care about one thing or will have a particular set of values when in fact that audience actually cares about something quite different.

Middle

The middle contains the meat of your presentation. Here you will explain the new ideas that will pique your audience's interest, tell the stories that will persuade them emotionally, and show them the spectacle that will move them. If the beginning of your presentation set the stage and drew them into the world where you'll be able to work your magic on them, the middle is where that magic actually happens.

The middle of your presentation is the place for most of your stories, supporting data, and persuasive arguments.

End

Remember those three main ideas we discussed in the last section? When you get to the end of the talk, it's important to give a quick recap of those ideas. The words and phrases you use here are often what an audience will remember most clearly about your talk. I give a slightly different point of view on this technique in the next section.

Salespeople would call the end of your presentation "the close," by which they mean it is the point at which they would get you to take out your wallet and pay for the thing they've been persuading you to buy. The end of your talk is a good place to briefly recall the points you've made, touch on the stories you've told, and reinforce the emotions you've stirred. And the salespeople are correct; the end of your talk is where you close the sale on the call to action—the change your talk set out to create. It is said that the biggest failure for most salespeople is the failure to actually ask the client to buy. If you don't ask for the action you want, you are far less likely to get it. If you don't demand commitment, you're risking failure for your talk.

Once you've closed the sale with a recap of ideas and a call to action, it's important to remind the audience of your name and to thank them. One way to thank an audience is to take a moment to acknowledge their applause and to make yourself available for questions or further discussions after the formal presentation has ended.

Another Three Parts

Another three-part formula that's important to ensuring that your presentation makes its point comes from a maxim I first heard in an old movie: "First you tell them what you're going to tell them, then you tell them, then you tell them what you told them."

What I'm Going to Tell You

"Telling them what you're going to tell them" means that, at the beginning of your talk, you let the audience in on what the talk is going to be about and how it's going to be structured. If I were giving a talk about creating powerful presentations, the first part might look like this:

"We're going to examine three main parts of creating any presentation, and I'll explain how to make sure each one has the maximum possible effect. First, we'll talk about honing your stated purpose for the talk. Then we'll talk about actually creating the presentation—the nuts and bolts of writing, building audio and visual support materials, and the like. Finally, we'll talk about the things you need to know in order to deliver that talk before an audience. OK, let's begin. . . ."

Now I'm Telling You

That was the setup. It could be more complicated—or not. Generally, simpler is better. You can convey more complicated concepts in speaker notes or handouts, but audiences can only remember so much. The rule of thumb is that they'll remember three main points from any particular talk, so it pays to keep the talk to just the most important three things you want them to take away.

In the setup I showed you in the preceding section, you'll note that there were to be three parts of the presentation: defining purpose, creating the talk, and delivering the talk.

I would follow the same three-part pattern with each of the three points I said I would make: "First, we're going to talk about defining our purpose." Then I would tell them a story with an emotional hook that drives home the importance of defining the purpose before beginning to create the talk and give them several quick techniques for clarifying their purpose. I would wind up that section of the talk with something like "So that's why it's so important to define the purpose for any presentation. Now, we'll move on to . . . " the second point of the talk. At the end of that segment, I'd once again tell them what I've told them so far. "And those are the basics of building your presentation. We covered X, Y, and Z techniques. At this point, we've talked about clarifying your purpose and building your talk [what I have told them so far]. Now it's time to talk about delivery."

Now You've Been Told

The third part of this pattern is the recap, or summary. When we listen to and watch a presentation, many of us get so caught up in the moment-to-moment experience that it's easy to forget what we've just been through. As the presenter, you can help. Keep in mind that your listeners are only going to remember three, perhaps four main points. But within each of those, there may be three or four other points, and if you recap each section fully, you can help them retain more.

The recap is about more than just helping your audience remember, though. You might recall from the discussion in earlier sections that the summary is also where you can drive home the emotional and logical arguments of your talk and make your call to action. Whether you want to enlist aid for a social cause, sell a product, generate investments in your project, or something else, the final section of the talk is when you'll ask the audience to take the action you are requesting.

Talks without a clear call to action are often dismissed: "Well, that was a lot of interesting information, but I'm not sure what the point was." Students hate it when they leave class wondering, "What was the point of all that?" If you're speaking to employees and paying for their time to listen to you, it is particularly important that they understand the point you're trying to make. Again, a clear call to action is essential. Lawyers in court know that they must make a clear request to the jury to "find in favor of my client" and that omitting something as simple as that clear call to action can cost them a case they would have won otherwise.

It's Always a Show

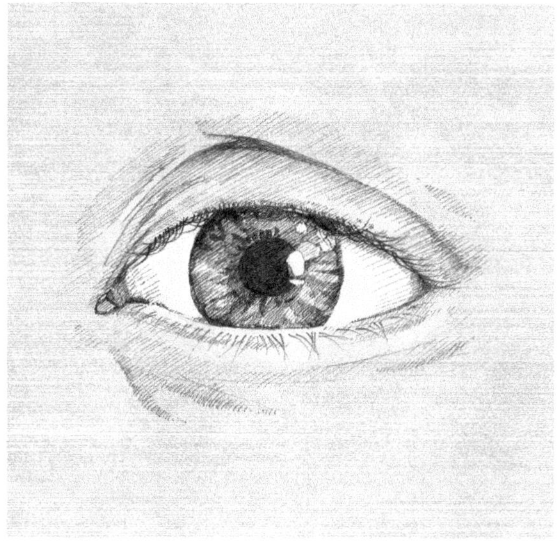

Chapter 5: It's Always a Show

Any time you're standing before a group, you are, in a sense, putting on a show. Since it's inescapable, you might as well make it a great show. I've spent my life creating great shows and learning about just how to do that. Here are a few of the most important things I've learned. You've already seen some of them in the preceding chapters, but they're important enough to bear repeating and expanding on.

Appeal to Five Senses

Different people respond to different kinds of sensual stimuli. Some of us are visually oriented, responding to colorful images, interesting compositions, and other visual elements. Others respond better to aural stimuli. Words, music, and the like move us more effectively and make an event memorable for us. Still others respond most strongly to kinesthetic stimuli. We like being touched or sensing movement, and that's why we describe memorable occasions as being "deeply moving." A great show (or sales pitch) uses as many different kinds of sensual stimuli as possible.

Use many methods to engage various senses. You can ask audiences to do things like raise their hands, stand up, sit down, look around, clap or chant, thus engaging them kinesthetically and aurally. When telling a story, make sure to include details about how things look, sound, and feel (and, possibly, how they smell and taste as well). Ask your audience to imagine a variety of sensory experiences: "Imagine for a moment that you're sitting on a warm tropical beach beneath a clear, starry sky, and you feel a salty, seaside breeze caressing your skin as you listen to the gentle waves caress the beach. As you walk toward your favorite seaside restaurant, enjoying the sights and sounds of the happy crowd, you can almost taste that cold cocktail. . . ." The words create the sensory experience.

Control Attention

A good showman is a master at directing a story line by controlling his or her audience's attention from moment to moment. Orchestrate your audience's attention consciously. It's important to always know where you want people to focus their attention and to be aware of that where their attention is. By controlling attention, you control your audience's experience of your presentation. When do you want people to look at your face, giving your words their full attention, and when do you want them to look at a splashy, emotionally evocative image on the screen? Should you be silent while they look at the screen or provide voice-over narration for actions or images on the screen? Are your images distracting from what you're saying by remaining up after you've moved on to other topics or by containing too much extraneous information or material that is too complicated? Map out how you will direct your audience's attention.

Create a Spectacle

What is spectacle, precisely? On one level, it simply means the visual portion of what you present to your audience. What do your slides look like? What does the overall picture look like, from moment to moment, during your talk?

On another level, you might think of spectacle as what the circus offers: spectacular stimulation of all your senses through the use of color, light, beautiful people, movement, and so on. Different kinds of shows demand different kinds of spectacle. A performance by Cirque du Soleil is spectacular because of its fantastically visual, maximally sensory, and amazingly stimulating sets, costumes, masks, and acrobatic skills. A one-man show, in which a single actor stands onstage in a pool of light, can be just as spectacular but probably uses relatively few visual elements to achieve its aims. In that case, it's the story, the vocal pyrotechnics, and the actor's presence that create the spectacle in the minds of the audience members. Still, shiny things tend to catch our attention. Things that move in interesting ways catch our attention. An interesting soundtrack can make a presentation more engaging and instantly conjure rich associations.

Let your imagination dream up multiple possibilities for making an impression on your audience through spectacle. If a picture is worth a thousand words, what would an animated picture be worth? True wizard presenters will go back to this part of their presentations again and again, always looking for ways to make their presentations more spectacular.

Use Rhythm

Have you ever attended a concert where the band played one song after another, all with a similar rhythm? It can become tedious. A great artist takes audiences on more of an emotional roller coaster, mixing driving fast rhythms with romantic slow ballads or interesting syncopated pieces that make the audience want to get up and dance. It's the same with presentations; rhythmic variety works best for keeping the audience engaged.

Most of us have habitual vocal patterns. We speak at a certain speed and with a certain set of inflection patterns that repeat again and again. However, when we're excited about something, those patterns change. And when we're bored with something, they change again. A good deal of our vocal character is defined by the rhythms we use most. To be an effective presenter, you need to be aware of the rhythms you use. You will want to consciously choose the times when you will slow down, when your language and voice will take on a poetic tone, or when you will speed up as you build excitement.

One way to become aware of your speech patterns is to record your talk when you rehearse and then listen to it, paying special attention to the rhythms. Another is to try delivering the whole talk with a particular rhythm—all the way through very fast, and then again very slowly—and thus discovering the specific places in the talk that work better at the different speeds.

Build Suspense

You've heard the term cliff-hanger. If you've read Dan Brown's novels, finding them almost impossible to put down, it's partly because each short chapter ends with a great cliff-hanger—a situation that arouses curiosity about what will happen next. I sometimes find myself binge-watching a TV series, unable to stop at the end of any particular episode, because the writers have structured the programs so that each episode ends with a moment that makes me feel I just have to know how the situation resolves—that is, a cliff-hanger.

If you can build a series of such moments into your presentation, creating questions that your listeners feel they need to know the answers to and then making them wait for the answers, you'll find that this kind of suspense works very well for holding their interest. In addition, when you resolve the tension you've created by building suspense, you're giving the audience an emotional reward, and they'll repay you handsomely for that gift, through their applause and their willingness to consider what you're asking them to do.

The Five-Act Play

Another way of organizing an experience is through the structure of the a five-act play. You might remember this structure from middle school English class. It's another system for breaking experiences into understandable parts and another useful guide to the elements of a presentation.

Opening Exposition

We're back to "Where is the audience when you begin?" What can you assume your listeners know, and what information do you need to provide so that they'll understand what you present later? How do you set the scene for the transformation you want them to make?

Rising Action

Rising action is part of the meat of your message. In drama, rising action takes place mainly in the form of a conflict between a protagonist hero and an antagonist villain. All of the actions are small parts of the larger action of the overall piece. In your presentation, rising action is the process of layering information about the problem you want your listeners to solve, working out small conflicts and addressing their objections, usually through stories or anecdotes, and thus moving the audience toward the big transition you want them to make.

Crisis

Rising action tends to build tension, to raise questions that require resolution, and to lead to a crisis—a moment at which a decision becomes necessary before anyone involved can move forward. Crisis points can be important to your presentations in two ways.

First, good presentations include stories, and one of the things that makes stories great is that cliff hangar moment when everything hangs in the balance and no one knows which way things will go. If you can find ways to build strong crisis moments into your stories, you'll have no difficulty holding your audience's interest.

Second, your presentation is, itself, a kind of story. Imagine your audience going home and telling their friends about your talk. "First, she told us all about X. Then she said there was a problem, because of Y and Z." And so the presentation becomes a story itself. It will pay you to consider the story that will be told about your presentation in the same way you consider the stories it contains. If that story has a strong crisis moment, chances are you've been successful with your presentation.

Climax

A climax is the moment when the dam of tension bursts and the crisis is resolved through action. The protagonist either wins or loses at the climactic moment. In a sale, it is the "sign on the dotted line" moment. In a story, it is often the moment when the protagonist changes, the moment when all the tension that has been built up through rising action is released. In most of the stories you tell during your presentations, you'll want this moment of climax to be one of satisfaction. Sometimes it will not be that, though. Sometimes it will be the moment of assured devastation, which only the audience's decision to act can avert.

When it comes to the overall structure of your presentation, the climax will be a moment of transformation, the moment when the audience makes a decision to change, to let go of an old belief or behavior and embrace a new one. The climax is, in short, the moment when you, as presenter, win or lose.

Denouement

In a story or dramatic piece, the denouement is the section after the climax during in which the author ties up all the loose ends from rising action questions that have not been resolved in the climax. Minor characters and plots are all resolved in ways consistent with the overall theme and message of the story. That theme or message is often stated explicitly at this point with a phrase like "and the moral of the story is . . . ."

During the denouement of a presentation, you will want to take a moment to make sense of the experience, turning information and action into meaning. If you have left loose ends in the form of facts presented without a specified purpose, or stories that have ended ambiguously, the denoument is where you'll make sure all of those elements are clarified. It's the time when you give your audience the payoff of feeling good about the decision you've led them to make.

That's the classical five-act structure. It's so prevalent throughout literature, drama, and many of our daily experiences that we come almost to expect it. When a particular experience leaves out one or more of the acts, we can be left feeling incomplete, and the experience becomes less definable, less memorable, and less persuasive. What does this expectation mean for you as a presenter? It means that you might want to use this five act checklist to check your presentations before you actually give them. Following the five act structure will help you make each of your talks more effective than it might have been otherwise.

Making the Show Great

I've spent my whole life creating shows, and it can be a lot of fun. Creating an experience to entrance, frighten, enlighten, or delight an audience is a very satisfying way to spend your time. But the true wizard presenter won't be creating an experience just to entertain. No, we want to both entertain and *transform* our audiences. Usually, the more entertaining a presentation is, the more memorable it will be. The more memorable it is, the more effective a presentation can be at transforming it's audience. The best shows actually change the lives of those who experience them.

Learning the things principles in this chapter can set you on the path to becoming a good showman. Remember, though, that every presentation, every show can be improved. We can always find ways to make our stories more emotionally evocative or to raise the level of the spectacle. Once you begin thinking about how shows actually work to move their audiences, you'll find that you learn more about that process with every show you see. So get out there and see as many shows as you can, and make sure you continue to learn from them. That way, you'll continue to improve your own presentations and will better understand why the presentations of others succeed or fail.

It's Always a Sale

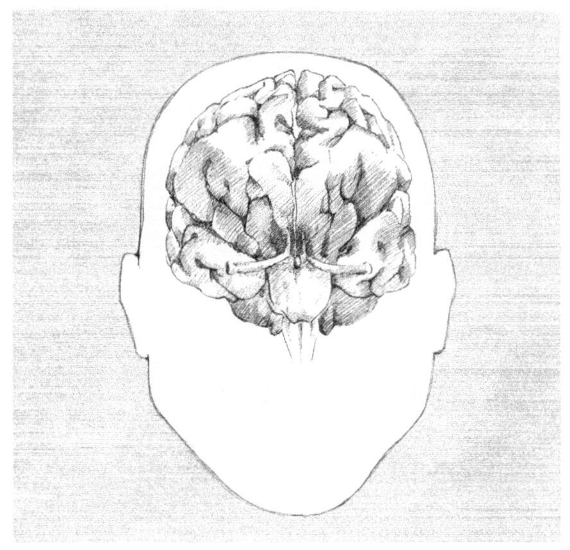

Chapter 6: It's Always a Sale

Of the metaphors that are useful in structuring a presentation, thinking of it as a sale is one of the most powerful. All sales have common elements, and many sales training programs sum them up with the acronym AIDAS. The letters stand for attention, interest, desire, action, and satisfaction.

Attention

The first step is to get a prospective buyer's attention. Ideally, you want to draw her attention to the thing you want her to buy, but that isn't always necessary. In effect, you're just directing her attention to the train of thought, the mental and emotional journey you have prepared for her.

As a speaker, you have a number of advantages when it comes to securing your audience's attention. One is the physical setup under which most presentations take place. You're standing in front, facing the members of the audience, who are all seated facing you. The physical setup and social norms dictate that they must give you their attention. Chances are that someone will give you a formal introduction, which further focuses the audience's attention.

The intensity of the audience's attention is quite another matter, though. If you don't open your presentation with something that grabs your listeners' attention right away, their focus will fade, and they'll begin daydreaming, texting, talking to their neighbors, or otherwise drifting away.

You can secure an audience's full attention in a number of ways. One of my favorites is to get audience members immediately involved in taking some sort of action related to the talk. Having them respond to a question you ask, clap in unison, stand up, chant something, or otherwise get themselves involved in the presentation, as a group, works wonderfully. It's great if you can come up with a way to relate the action to what you want the talk to accomplish, but you don't necessarily have to. You just need the action to focus your listeners' attention on you and the presentation, taking their minds off all the other things they could be focusing on.

Loud noises, explosions, or flashy images also attract attention. If you can find a way to surprise your audience right at the start of a presentation, that will grab their attention. The device can be something as simple as asking them a surprising question that they will really care about answering. Perhaps something like "If I could tell you the moment you will die, would that interest you?"

My friend Marco Tempest used to have quite a business built around this "getting the audience's attention" moment for CEOs and marketing directors at the general sessions of huge corporate meetings or conferences. Marco would create a digital countdown that would play throughout the huge ballroom on dozens of screens. A few minutes before the meeting was to begin, lights that had been swirling about the audience would move down toward the stage, and the images on all the screens except those at the front of the room would fade. A solitary figure (Marco) carrying a brilliant orb of light would walk out onto the stage, in front of the last beats of the countdown. A flash of light would appear on the screen, and Marco would throw the light in his hand out at the audience, where it would circle for a moment and then return to his hands. He would split it in two and toss one of the parts into the giant screen that filled the whole stage. There, the light would streak around the screen and then explode into an image—usually the company's logo or the emblem of the conference. He would split off another orb and toss that into the screen. Another streak and explosion, and the theme for the meeting would appear in giant letters. Finally, he would toss the last orb into the giant screen, where it would explode in a ball of fire. At the center of the fire, the audience would see the silhouette of a man or woman. The silhouette would turn and walk toward one edge of the screen, just as a thundering voice would announce, "Ladies and gentlemen, Joanna Smith!" As the silhouette reached the edge of the screen, it would seemingly melt right through the edge, and the real person would step into a pool of light right there, seemingly having just walked out of the screen. She had the rapt attention of all in the room.

You might not have the budget nor the need for such a huge spectacle just to get the attention of your audience, but this example should get you thinking of ways to generate the anticipation and attention you want to kick off your presentations.

Interest

The second step in any sales process is to develop your client's interest in the thing you want them to buy. This process will be different for each talk and for each audience you speak to. If you are speaking to an audience of salespeople, you might appeal to their interests by including stories about sales and marketing or why sales are so important to their company. Engineers will be interested in technology and scientific details. You get the picture; each audience will have its own unique set of interests. But there are certain things that capture almost everyone's interest: hot topics from the news, sports, pets, families. If you can create associations between the thing you want to get this particular audience to do and the interests they already have, you will be on your way to building a successful presentation for them.

Having a firm command of all the features of whatever you're selling will help you develop interest in your product or cause among different types of clients. If you are selling a car, automotive enthusiasts will be interested in power, handling, and gas mileage, while soccer moms will have a different set of interests for the same product. The more you know about your particular cause and how it can relate directly to the lives of a particular set of listeners, the greater chance you have of keeping their interest.

Desire

Once potential buyers become interested, it is time to stimulate their desire for the thing you want them to buy or the action you want them to embrace. How will this particular thing make their life or their world better? Will doing what you want or having the thing you are selling improve their image of themselves? Will it help bring them closer to the people they love? Will it simplify their work and make them more effective at whatever their job is?

Benefits

Thinking of what you are selling not as a thing but as a bundle of benefits for the members of the audience—a package of ways to dramatically improve their lives—will help you know how to develop their desire for it.

Involvement

Another great tool for developing desire is involvement. When you wander into an automotive showroom and look at several different models, the salesperson knows she can get you to really want one of them. How? By having you sit in the car and then take it for a test drive. At that point, you are involved and the desire quotient goes way up! How can you get your audience involved with what your talk is selling them?

Action

Once you have the client wanting what you're selling, you need to move him to take an action. If you are selling a product, the action would be either to take the next step toward a sale or to actually make the purchase. When salespeople fail to make most of their sales, it is usually because they fail to ask the client to take action. It's the same with a talk. If you want your talk to succeed, you need to ask your audience to take an action at the end of the talk.

There are many whole books on the art of closing a sale, and they make for interesting reading. In my experience, a direct approach is usually best. "If I've convinced you of the importance of X, Y, and Z, and I hope I have, now is the time for you to act. Here's what you can do." Sometimes it can help to offer a binary choice: "Now is the time to decide, will you sit back and allow A, B, and C to happen, or will you be the ones to take actions X, Y, and Z and make this a better world for all of us?"

Whatever your particular X, Y, and Z actions might be, it's important that you make them specific actions that your audience can take, and the sooner they can do it, the better. "Now is the time. If you're with me, please turn on your phone right now, and send an e-mail to xyz@take-actionnow.com." Or, "Don't forget to sign one of our petitions on your way out." I think you get the idea. When you give an audience an action they can start on right away, you'll find that you get a much larger overall response than if you assign them something vague or something that they can only do after they get back home.

Satisfaction

Great salespeople don't see their job as being finished when the client signs on the dotted line. If you make a purchase, they want to make certain you are satisfied with the sale and, ideally, that you signify that satisfaction in a way that will make you feel that you're committed to it. If you can get your listeners to tell others, right away, about what a great talk they've just heard or what a great product or service they've just discovered, they are far more likely to remain committed to that position than if they simply go home and get on with their lives. Great salespeople don't just make sales, they create clients and whole networks of clients—people who will buy from them again and again and will refer their friends.

In the case of a presentation, creating a client means encouraging follow-up. Get your audience members to go to your website, send you e-mail, or post to your social media pages in order to continue the discussion. When they do reach out to you in one of those ways, make sure they receive a response. The response they get should be positive. By responding positively to their comment, you're making them part of your community and greatly increasing the chance that they'll join your cause.

Creating Transformational Experiences

Chapter 7: Creating Transformational Experiences

Basic data and bare-bones logic all by themselves make for boring presentations. Tell stories in order to draw your audience in and to bypass their logical, linear objections. Stories provide vicarious experience, and, as all true wizards know, experience is what changes people. Actual interactive experiences can be even more powerful than vicarious ones, so the best speakers find ways to include those, too.

Using the Power of Stories

Some people theorize that we can only think clearly about experiences once we have distilled them into words. Others tell us that we only make sense of events once we turn those words into stories. Stories are the way that our minds make sense of the world. Stories evoke our emotions, and they tend to be what we remember.

Stories Create Mild Trance

A little-known effect of listening to a story is that the experience puts us into a light trance. You've experienced this type of trance if you've found yourself deeply involved in a great book or a show on television and failed to hear your family members talking with you. If you're like me, you might have to be called to dinner several times before you even hear the call. You are so buried in the world of the story that you're no longer really conscious of your everyday world. That is trance, and you'll find that the audiences at your presentations often fall into a mild trance state.

One of the things we know about trance is that under its influence, we become suggestible. When we are in a trance state, we accept and do things without the interference of our rational mind. Though it is true that a hypnotist can't make you do something you really don't want to do, you have to not want to do that thing at a fairly deep level in order to resist the hypnotist's command. As a true wizard and a power presenter, then, it's important for you to realize that you have the ability to issue commands and that your audience may simply accept them, to a degree that you might not be used to experiencing in everyday life. If your cause is just and important, you're completely justified in using this power.

Stories Engage Emotions

The best presentations are designed to change those who experience them. People are changed and people make decisions through emotion. Ninety-nine percent of decisions are purely emotional, and the rational mind only kicks in to justify the decision after it has already been made. Stories stir the emotions. Audiences identify with the protagonist of a story, and if something great happens to that person, they feel great. If something terrible happens, then they'll feel terrible—or outraged or whatever else your telling of the story is designed to make them feel. Your presentation can use imagery, rhythm, vocal dynamics, and other elements to enhance that emotion.

Therefore, if you want your presentation to be remembered, use stories to make your points. If you want your logic to be accepted, wrap it in a story!

Creating Interactive Experiences

Even better than a story we hear is one that we actually participate in. These are interactions. When a speaker involves audience members directly in her presentation, making them characters in the story she is creating for them, they find themselves much more deeply attached to and emotional about that story than one they have only heard rather than participated in. The story becomes more immediate. Instead of something that happened to someone else sometime in the past, it is happening to me, right now. It's hard not to be engaged in that!

Another thing that happens when people have experiences together is they begin to feel more like a group. Rather than an audience made up of lots of individuals, you begin to create a kind of tribal mind. Great speakers at political rallies and in large religious groups make use of this group feeling to great advantage. You can use it, too.

One way to generate direct interaction is just to ask for it. "Whenever I ask ,'Can we do it?' I need you to shout, 'Yes we can!'" Another is to ask people to stand in the audience or come to the stage and take a role. "If you could just stand here and hold this, and whenever I say X, you'll do Y. Got it?" When you do enlist the aid of an audience member, it's important for you to realize that you have made them a special representative of all the others in the audience and so it's important that you treat them well. Treat them badly, and you'll lose the audience. Yet another way to get involvement is just to ask for a response to a question. "Give me a show of hands. How many of you took a bus to get here? How many drove their own cars?" Any of these actions will get and keep your audience involved.

Attention Creates Experience

As a stage director, one of my most important jobs is to make sure the audience knows where to look. When I work with magicians, controlling the audience's attention is even more important. It's the same with your presentations.

Audiences can pay attention to exactly one thing at a time. If you give them multiple possible attention points, you will confuse and lose them. For example, if you present your audience members with a slide or other visual that is so complex that it will take them more than a few seconds to read or understand it, then continue speaking before they have completely absorbed the information on the slide, their attention will not be on what you are saying. Great presenters make sure they control where their audience's attention will be at all times throughout the presentation, first on the speaker, then on a visual, and then back on the speaker. While it's okay to narrate a slide, you need to be aware that when you are doing that, the audience's attention will be fully on the slide.

You can design your graphics so that they are only visible at full intensity during the time you want attention to be on the graphic and will then fade or blur out. You can learn to take the stage back from your slide by moving, raising your voice, asking a question that demands an answer, or any one of a hundred other ways. The time to think about all this is when you are still designing the experience.

If you want to become a real wizard at power presenting, try out as many of these different techniques in front of as many different audiences as possible. Some techniques will work and some will fail. Different techniques work for different people, and they work differently for different audiences. You won't know which techniques work best for you until you've tried them.

Designing Experiences

We've all designed experiences for others. If you've planned a date or a party, you've designed an experience. First, you'll have a reason for creating the experience. Perhaps you want to celebrate your friend or begin a romantic relationship or set the basis for a continuing business relationship.

Once you know what and who the experience is for, the next step in planning involves creating the framework. When and where will the experience start? How long will it go on? How will it end? Who will be invited?

Once you've chosen the framework, you begin filling in the experience. Sometimes we start with the end in mind. At a birthday party, this might be a climax of serving the candle-laden cake, followed by the opening of gifts. On a date, perhaps you want to build up to a kiss outside your date's front door. Once you know where you want the experience to lead, you can fill in the other parts. You already know when and where it will begin, but how will the experience itself start? Will there be flowers? An awkward greeting? Will there be drinks before dinner, or not? Will there be entertainment? If so, what kind? Will you be the one entertaining, or will you be sharing an entertainment someone else creates—for example, a play, concert, or movie? What sort of mood do you want to create? How will you do that?

Performers—magicians, comedians, and others—create experiences through their performances all the time. One of the things they have to learn, which separates the pros from the amateurs, is what to do when events take an unexpected course. Sometimes there will be hecklers. Sometimes the audience doesn't feel the same way that you do about the material you've planned. How will you react? Do you have options planned in case things don't work the way you had expected? Anticipating contingencies should always be part of your planning process.

For example, when you're doing a presentation for a group you don't know well, you might find out that they don't have the basic knowledge they need in order to understand the talk you have planned. I can imagine an application developer being asked to talk about his process and preparing a talk all about how the audience members can use a particular language or interface in the course of their work, assuming they use the same tools he does. When he arrives, he might find that the audience is made up of marketing executives with no programming experience at all, and who are therefore completely unable to understand or relate to the coding references he plans to use in the talk. If you're that presenter, how do you cope? Do you have a repertoire of other examples that can get your point across and that they will understand?

Or perhaps you discover that the members of your audience are actually hostile to the main idea of your talk. Perhaps you're a world-famous adventurer who has been asked to come and describe your adventures. You've decided to tell the story of your last big-game safari, hunting rare predators on the savanna in Africa. When you arrive, you discover the audience is made up of conservationists and animal rights activists who will be appalled that anyone might consider hunting wild animals of any kind, let alone potentially endangered species. How will you adjust? Have you planned for that eventuality?

Evaluating Your Design

Once you've filled in all the blanks, deciding what words and stories your audience will hear and the images they will see, it's time to go back and look over what you've created.

This is the time to ask yourself some questions. Is your purpose clear throughout the presentation? Does the process you've designed for the audience to experience actually support your purpose, moving listeners from a clear starting point to a clear ending? Have you made use of the sales principles that you've learned, to ensure that they buy in to what you're trying to achieve? Have you built in a highly entertaining element of showmanship?

One of the best lessons I ever got was from my acting teacher for a Shakespeare class in college. We had spent several weeks working on a particular scene, making sure we really understood all the language and all the different action beats of the scene and learning to really listen to and act on one another's characters. The work was good, and we were rightfully proud of it. The teacher was, too, and he let us know as much. "You've done really good work on this scene. Congratulations. I have only one more question for you: Is this really the best you're capable of? Are there no more exciting choices you might be able to make for each moment of the scene, if you were to go back and look at it again? In short, is there nothing left that you could improve?"

Of course, the answer to that question, if we were honest, was "no." Every performance—even the best—can be improved.

Therefore, in the spirit of making your presentation the best it can be, I challenge you to ask yourself, "OK, how can I make this clearer? More coherent? More emotionally involving? More persuasive?" Can you make the stories stronger? State your main points more clearly? Have you checked every logical assumption to make sure it is bulletproof? You won't be able to answer these questions until you've completed a first full draft of your presentation, but once you have, that's the best time to make improvements.

At this point, you've completed the design of your presentation. You have created the logic, collected the stories, designed interactive experiences for your audience, collected or created the visuals that will support you, and considered just how you will guide your audience's attention through the experience. That's a lot, but you're not done yet. An architect's job is not done when she has created a blueprint but when she's made sure that the building plan is fully realized in a physical structure. Sometimes those buildings don't turn out completely as the architect imagined them in the blueprints. It's the same for a presenter. Having a great design is important, but it doesn't guarantee a great presentation. That's the subject of our next section.

Delivering the Experience

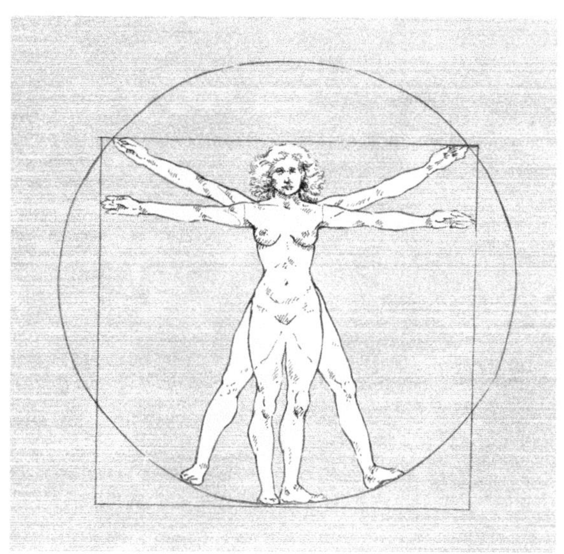

Chapter 8: Delivering the Experience

Once you've planned out the experience you want to give, the presentation that will transform your audience in just the way you want them to change, it's time to deliver it. Up until now, the presentation process has been an internal one. You've thought and dreamed of what you want your talk to do, and you've planned the experience that you hope will accomplish that goal. But you have not, as yet, made contact. If you've done all the necessary homework, this is the really exciting and fun part. If you haven't, well, your terror is well founded.

Rehearsal

If you've ever watched Steve Jobs deliver a keynote at a major product launch event, you were probably impressed by just how comfortable he looked. He was dressed in jeans and a turtleneck, and his tone was always conversational, almost as though he were speaking off the cuff, improvising as he went. Jobs's comfort level inspired comfort in his audiences. No one ever worried that he would lose his place, go off script, or otherwise leave them hanging. What a gifted presenter!

In fact, Jobs was always thoroughly rehearsed. Every moment of each keynote was planned, rehearsed, re-planned, re-rehearsed, and then run with full technical support, again and again. Aides would give notes, suggest improvements to a slide or the script, suggest adjustments to line readings, and so on. A friend who has worked at Apple for many years once told me that Jobs would often spend a whole week with his team to prepare for a single hour-long presentation. Only after using that comprehensive rehearsal process to truly master the presentation could he feel the confidence, the comfort level to deliver the talk. Rehearsal is one of the great keys to delivering truly powerful presentations. Winging it is courting failure.

It's a very poor presenter indeed who reads his or her presentation from the slides. The message you're sending is "don't look at me," which is only a small step away from "don't listen to this." If this is the kind of presentation you've planned, you might as well just send the slide deck and stay home yourself. You'll only alienate those who might otherwise be interested in the material you're presenting.

Basic Stagecraft

Whether you're on a large formal stage at a corporate meeting or in a smaller lecture hall on a college campus, paying attention to crucial aspects of stage management can make a big difference in the way your presentation is received.

The Stage

Every speaking situation has certain common elements with regard to staging. Most of the time, you, the speaker, will be facing your audience, with all or most of the audience seated directly in front of you. Sometimes you'll find yourself in a "half surround" situation, where the audience is arrayed around the stage, so some people are on either side of you as well as directly in front of you.

If you're using graphics on a screen to support your talk, the screen might be directly behind and above you, or it might be off to one side, or there may be multiple screens.

Sometimes you'll have a microphone and sound system. Sometimes the venue may have separately controlled stage and theater lighting. Whatever the case, as you rehearse, you'll want to tailor your presentation to the specific situation in that venue.

To optimize your presentation, you'll need to be able to communicate clearly and efficiently with stage managers and technicians, in language that they understand. Toward that end, here is a brief glossary of stage terms:

Stage right: The part of the stage to your right as you stand at the center of the stage while facing the audience.

Stage left: The part of the stage to your left as you face the audience.

Upstage: The part of the stage behind you when you're facing the audience. In earlier eras, stages were raked, which means that they were higher at the back than at the front, allowing audiences, who were often seated on a flat floor, to see better. Even though it is now rare to encounter a raked stage, the terminology persists.

Downstage: You guessed it: the part of the stage in front of you when you stand in the center, facing the audience; the part of the stage that is closest to the audience.

Something *coming in* means something coming down, while something *going out* means something going up. Most stages have pipes, lighting bars, scenery, and other items suspended above them. If someone calls out that a light bar is "coming in," they expect you to get out of the way in order to avoid the bar hitting you.

The "in," "out," "up" and "down" terminology can be confusing. For example, if a piece of scenery has been flown in and is hovering just above the stage, the instruction to "take it up" really means to swing it upstage, toward the back of the stage, not to fly it back "out," up into the air. For the most part, you won't have a lot of use for the "in" and "out" terminology, but you will often be asked to "move upstage just a bit" or to move something "a couple of feet to the left," which is assumed to mean "stage left" when you're on the stage. Learn and get used to basic stage directions, and you'll save time and get better results when you deal with stage managers, directors, and lighting technicians.

Crew

If you're on a program with other speakers or entertainers, you'll most likely be dealing with stage managers, directors, lighting crew, sound crew, stagehands, and others. You are, in effect, part of a theatrical production.

Keep in mind that each of these people is a contributor to the overall effect of your presentation. Remember that purpose you defined for yourself when designing the talk? Each one of these people has the power to either enhance your chances of achieving that purpose, that goal—or to destroy your chances completely. Make friends with each of them. Each one is a specialist, with knowledge of the stage, lights, sound equipment, or whatever else is within their purview, knowledge that you probably do not have. The speaker who respects his support crew will be vastly more successful than the one who treats them poorly. Stage technicians tend to take great pride in their knowledge and abilities, and they'll appreciate it if you notice the great job they are doing on your behalf. If you take the time to appreciate them and their work, your life as a presenter will be greatly enhanced.

One more note about acknowledging your helpers: It's natural to take time with the crew and staff before your talk in order to work out all the details you need to handle before you set foot onstage. A true professional will take time after she's done onstage, after that standing ovation, to seek out and thank each of the crew members who helped make the talk a success. The stagehand dragging a table onto the stage today might well become the talent director or producer for the next event you want to get booked for. Leave him with a good impression!

Staging Your Talk

Too often, beginning presenters fail to consider basic staging for their talks. They make easily avoidable errors, such as standing directly in front of the screen, thus blocking the view of the slides they are talking about. Other times, they might anchor themselves behind a podium and never move. That might be useful if you're worried about snipers, but it doesn't help you get your message across!

Here is some basic staging information you should consider:

1. Stand still most of the time when you're actually speaking, and move during the pauses between the lines of your talk.

2. Face your audience most of the time, either head on or at a slight angle. If you want to look at or point to a screen or another object that's slightly behind you, try to do so from the side, with most of your body still facing front.

3. It's okay to deliver much of your talk from one place, but it's even better if you can stage it so that you deliver different portions from different places. Prime locations are beside the screen on either side and also further downstage to the right, left, and center, as long as you're not blocking people's view of the slides or other visual aids and you're not hiding yourself from any part of the audience by standing behind a podium, stacks of speakers, or other objects.

4. If you're speaking for an American or European audience, your listeners will be used to reading from left to right and from the top to the bottom of the page. They will therefore have certain subconscious emotional associations with different sorts of movement and placement on the stage. By and large, the center of the stage will be the most powerful, commanding spot for a performer or speaker. Performers standing still at stage right will engender a warmer response; the audience will respond to them as more friendly, warm, happy people than their counterparts standing stage left. Stage directors make use of this knowledge when they create their stage pictures, placing their "good guy" heroes stage right when they confront their "bad guy" opponents standing stage left. Spooky stories might be better delivered from stage left; heartwarming ones, from stage right.

When you first enter a new space, take a few minutes to look at the stage from the audience. The arrangement of and relationship between screens, speakers, scenery, and human presenters creates a picture. Sometimes there will be a proscenium framing the scene, sometimes not. As you look at the stage and imagine yourself on it, how would you feel about yourself (as the presenter) standing in different places with regard to the screen (or screens)? Are there places you need to avoid, so you won't block the screens from some of the audience? Places where, should you stand there, it might make some parts of the audience uncomfortable because the overall picture becomes unbalanced? Where will you need to stand when you want to take the audience's focus? Where and how should you stand in order to give focus to the screen or to another person? Think about all these things as you consider how you'll move during this particular talk.

As a general rule, when considering your movement on a stage, you'll want to try for just a few moves during the talk, with each one creating a new stage picture and each one building your own energy and status as a part of that picture, so that your biggest moment will be at the climax of your talk. Whenever possible, actually arrange to rehearse on the stage, with the slides running, the microphone on, and so forth. Sometimes that's not possible, and in those cases, it might help to rehearse the whole presentation in your head.

Rehearse How You'll Control Attention

You'll recall from earlier sections of this book that it's extremely important to control an audience's attention. Most people can only give conscious attention to one thing at a time. If you allow people's attention to wander, they'll lose track of what you're trying to get across.

Now is a time to reconsider presentation technique and attention control. At any given moment during your talk, you'll want the audience's attention either on you and what you're saying or on a visual aid. It can't be in both places, or at least, not for long. How will you control where people's attention will go? It's easy to know you should do that, but how?

One way is by pausing. When you bring up a new slide, if you turn slightly to look at the slide and then pause and take a deep breath while the audience absorbs what is on that slide, you can then start speaking again as you turn back to the audience, and their attention will come back to you. If you choose that moment to move across the stage, you'll get even more interest.

You can enhance this effect by having your slides come up at full brightness for a few seconds and then dim, blur, or otherwise fade into the background. You can also call extra attention to a particular slide by pointing, building animation into the slide, or using sound effects when the slide appears. Effective use of slides in a presentation is much like a dialogue between the speaker and the screen, with the audience always knowing where to look and easily following the flow of attention.

Let me warn you that if a slide is complex enough that it will take more time to read than it takes you to inhale and release a deep breath, it's probably too complex to work well in the context of your talk. I've coached many science students on their presentations, and this is an extremely difficult thing for them to grasp. They've spent so much time doing experiments and building data sets in order to reach their conclusions, that it's very difficult for them not to want to show off all that work, yet it can make a presentation almost impossible to follow.

So, please, save more complex details for handouts or other materials you can provide to interested listeners for reference after your talk has ended. If the audience is busy trying to read your slide as you go on speaking, they won't hear what you're saying.

When I make a presentation, I ask that the lights in the auditorium be bright enough that I can see my audience and that there not be a bright spotlight in my eyes. I communicate this to the crew during my rehearsal time with them. That way I can see where the audience is looking at all times. I can see where people's attention is and, if necessary, redirect it. Remember, presenting is an interactive activity, not one that flows in only one direction, so plan the ways you can optimize that interactivity before you actually step in front of the audience. Prepare in advance so that you can be flexible during the actual presentation.

Deliverying the Presentation

After all your hard work, the magic moment arrives; you are about to "stand and deliver." This, of course, is the real test of your presentation, and if you've properly prepared and rehearsed, you are fully positioned to succeed in a big way. The following sections detail a few things to attend to at the time of your talk.

Warm Up

Most people find that speaking in front of a group gives them a kick of adrenaline. You can choose to interpret this either as stage fright or as excitement. It's up to you. My friend Jeff McBride likes to tell his students, "We all get butterflies. The trick is teaching them to fly in formation."

One of the ways to train your butterflies is to give yourself the gift of short physical and vocal warm-ups before you step in front of an audience. You needn't do the warm-ups just before you walk on; sometimes conditions don't allow that. But you should try to complete some physical and vocal exercises within a half hour of the time you go onstage.

Why Warm Up?

Performers of all kinds know the value of warm-ups. Musicians tune their instruments and play scales and etudes before their performance. Vocalists do their vocal exercises. Dancers work out at a ballet barre for half an hour or more before they take the stage. All of these warm-ups are the equivalent of tuning an instrument. No one wants to hear a concert in which all the instruments are out of tune. As a presenter, your voice and body are your instruments, so if you want to be sure you'll hit the stage at your best, a warm-up is the way to go.

Sample Warm-up

Here's a basic warm-up technique I like to use. It's easy to remember, because you use your body as the map.

Start with your head and face. Stretch your face and turn it up to the ceiling as far as you can, also making it as long as you can by dropping your jaw. Then drop your head down to your chest, scrunching up your face and stretching the back of your neck. I think of it as making my face as long as I can and then as small as I can.

Now turn your head as far to one side as you can, then to the other side. Repeat. Shake your head from side to side. Blow out your lips to make a noise like a horse snorting. Smile. Frown. Make a crybaby face and then a big laugh face.

Next, move down to your shoulders and chest. Lift the shoulders up toward your ears. Really stretch them up—and then drop them. Do it several times. Now make circles with your shoulders. Lift them up, pull them forward, pull them downward, and then back. Go as far as you can in each direction, and do the full rotation several times. Then reverse it; instead of up, forward, down and back, you'll move your shoulders up, backward, down and forward. Repeat that a few times.

Next, try circles with your rib cage. Most people have difficulty isolating their rib cage, but it can be done! First, shift it as far front as you can, then backward. Repeat. Then try side to side. Right, center, left, center. Then try making a big circle; front, right, back, center. Do a couple of full rotations, then reverse the circle.

Now move the sequence down to your hips. Front, back, front back. Left, right, left, right. Then big circles. Imagine standing inside a barrel that is just as high as your hips, imagining that your hips stay in touch with the rim of the barrel as they circle, first to the right for several times around, then to the left.

Next, place your hands on your knees, bending your knees enough to make that possible. Rotate your knees in circles to the right and to the left.

Now stand on one leg and rotate the foot of the other leg. If you need to, hold onto a chair or place your hand against a wall to help you balance. Do the same action for both feet.

You've now gone from top to bottom, stretching and flexing all the major joints. Now it's time to make sure your spine is fully in the game. Start by stretching your hands as high above your head as you can, while looking up. Then drop your hands forward and let them slowly pull you downward, one vertebra at a time, until your whole body is hanging forward. Depending on how limber you are, your fingers may be touching the floor or they may only reach as far as your knees. If they aren't touching the floor, try bending your knees until they do. Breathe in and out a few times while you're in that position, and then start rolling back up your spine, stacking one vertebra on top of the next, starting at the very bottom, until you're standing upright again. Repeat the whole sequence, starting with stretching your hands upward.

At this point, you might want to do several squats in order to make sure the big muscles in your legs are working fully.

Now that you have stretched and warmed up most of your major joints and muscles, it's time to check on your voice. Do you recall my earlier suggestion that you take some voice lessons? If you've done that, you probably know a basic vocal warm-up. If so, go ahead and use it. If not, try this one:

Stand with your feet parallel, at shoulder width. Pay attention to your breath, which you should be able to feel by placing your hands on your abdomen, just above your navel. Don't force it, but gradually deepen your breathing; your hands should move in and out as you breathe. Open up as much of your lung capacity as possible.

After a minute or two of paying attention and deepening your breath, begin to let your exhales include an audible sigh—just the sound "ah" escaping with your breath, just enough to warm up your vocal chords. Do that for several breaths, then gradually let the sound harden as you control it into a hard and long "ahhhhh" sound and then an "Aum" sound, which can heighten awareness of all the possible resonance in your vocal chambers.

The "Aum" can include all of the possible vowel sounds a person can make and resonate all around the vocal cavity. It begins with a flat "a" sound as in the word "at." That tends to resonate on the front of the tongue. The flat "a" sound shifts smoothly to the sound of "ah," a bit further back on the lower surface of your mouth. "Ah" becomes "oh" and moves a bit further toward the back of the mouth, and up just a bit. The "oh" becomes "owe" and moves further up, to the top of the vocal cavity but still in the back. This shifts to an "oo" sound up on the hard palate and then through a very narrow "ew" sound at the front of the hard palate and then finally to "ee" at the front of the mouth, and then hum, "mmmm" as the mouth closes. Try it; I'm sure you'll be able to feel the resonance of your voice within the different locations within your head.

At this point, some people like to sing a bit or just vocalize up and down a scale. Others like to hum while making chewing motions with their mouths, which helps them further warm up the resonance of their voice.

Before ending the vocal section of your warm-up, it's important to work your articulation. Your tongue, teeth, and lips form all of the consonants in our language, and having them well warmed up will prevent you from tripping over your words when you start your talk. I find that traditional tongue twisters work best; for example, try several repetitions of each of the following phrases, saying them faster and faster as you repeat them:

"Bimini bomini, Mimini momini" (repeat)

"Ta da sa, Ta da za" (repeat)

"Typical topical, Typical topical, Topeka, Topeka" (repeat)

"Seven silly sisters sat sewing in the sand." (repeat)

While doing tongue twisters, over-enunciate as much as possible, going faster and faster. Having done that, you'll find that you've trained your tongue, teeth, and lips to enunciate clearly, and you won't need to think very much about enunciation as you present your talk.

You've now done a thorough warm-up of your body and voice. I like to add one step that helps my get my energy opened up full throttle before I hit the stage. Here's how it goes:

Stand, once again, with your feet at about shoulder width, parallel to one another, with your knees slightly bent and your arms hanging loosely at your sides. Your body should be loose and comfortable, with your head hanging a bit forward. Your weight should be on the balls of your feet. Keeping the balls of your feet on the floor, begin a running-in-place motion, alternately lifting each heel and then slapping it down on the floor. As you increase the intensity of this action, your thighs will begin to shake. As you increase the shaking of your thighs, your torso will start torso shaking, too. Allow the shaking action to grow and take over your whole body, moving up from your feet to your knees, to thighs, to belly, to chest and arms (really shake your arms as the shaking moves up your torso). When the action reaches your belly, allow a low growling sound to come from your mouth. As your shaking arms slowly lift, let the shaking continue to move up up through your shoulders, neck, and head, and out the top of your head. As this happens, your growl will increase in pitch and volume until the whole action feels as though it is shooting out the top of your head, at which point it will end. You may feel slightly out of breath for a moment, and your heart rate will have increased. You should also feel fully alert, energized, and ready to bound onto the stage and dazzle your audience with the best presentation they've ever experienced!

You don't have to do this exercise immediately before you go onstage. Do it in your dressing room or other private space backstage, up to half an hour before you are scheduled to start the talk.

Frame Your Talk with a Strong Introduction

Usually, when you give a presentation at a conference or other event, someone introduces you. In meetings or private pitch sessions, that may not be the case, but often it is, and when someone does introduce you, it is important that they do so in a way that will be beneficial for what follows. Many of the clients I've worked with recently are magicians who have turned to public speaking. If we don't provide our hosts with a specific introduction, we're likely to get something like the following:

"Our next speaker is a magician from Las Vegas, so be sure to hold onto your wallet!"

Even though the humor may put the audience in a good mood, an introduction like that sends the message that the speaker is not to be trusted. The speaker starts the presentation in a hole he must climb out of before he can get the audience fully focused on the content of his talk. If you take full responsibility for communicating to the person who will introduce you the introduction should go easily and as planned. In the rare event you find yourself sabotaged by your introducer, you should take a moment or two to give yourself the introduction you had planned. "OK, we've had a good laugh, but in fact, I'm not here to (do the terrible thing they suggested you might do). Let me tell you just a bit about who I am, and why you might want to hear about what I have come to tell you." Then give them the two or three sentences that you had wanted the person introducing you to give.

A good introduction should answer three basic questions: Who are you? What are you going to talk about? Why should the audience care? Here's an introduction that I sometimes use:

"Your next speaker comes to us from the world of show business. Trained as a performer and director, he went on to produce and manage some of the world's great shows, from Broadway to Las Vegas and all around the world. Tonight, he shares the secrets and stories of wizards from legend and history as detailed in his latest book, *The Wizard's Way*. Prepare to be transformed! Please welcome Tobias Beckwith."

To make sure that this is the introduction that will actually be used, I prepare a 4" x 6" card with the words printed in the largest, clearest font you can find, completely filling the card. At the top is my name and a thumbnail photo of myself. (You should also include pronunciation information if your name is likely to be pronounced incorrectly.) When I hand the card to the person before the event begins, I tell them it's very important that they use just these words to introduce me, because my talk will refer back to the introduction.

I strongly advise you to create your own introduction card. When writing an introduction for yourself, keep it short. Three sentences is about right, but it could be one sentence more or less. The introduction should be honest, and it should provide some sense of why the audience would want to hear what you have to tell them. Try to keep the sentences and words as short and easy to recognize as possible, to help the person avoid mispronouncing or stumbling over words while introducing you. The tone of the introduction should match the tone of the beginning of your talk. If you're starting with humor, it's okay to use humor in the introduction. Otherwise, probably not.

You can create a different introduction card each time you speak, to accommodate varying circumstances. For example, if the person introducing you is a friend, you might include a phrase like "I've known Cindy for over a decade, so I know you're in for a treat." Each group is likely to be impressed by different aspects of your background. And if you deliver several types of presentations, tailoring your introduction to the type of presentation might be useful.

The introduction is like a frame for your presentation. Just as different kinds of frames can enhance or detract from the effect of a painting, so different introductions can enhance or detract from your presentation.

Take Command of the Stage

Many inexperienced presenters begin speaking in the first moment they step onto the stage. The audience has not had time to see and connect with the presenter, so the first sentence or two end up being lost while the audience tries to absorb their first impressions of the speaker. Rushing in this way sends a message to the audience that the presenter is not in control, not in command of the presentation, and the audience tunes out. Don't let that happen to you.

Here's how to take the stage as a true wizard, a power presenter would: Walk on with good, strong energy. Remember that you own the room. Stop, and take a moment to look over the audience members. Nod to them, and say thank you to the person who introduced you. Then stand tall, take a deep breath, and begin.

Now put into practice all we discussed earlier about making connections and building rapport. You've rehearsed your talk many times, so you don't need to worry about the talk itself. Your sole object is to sway the audience members to change, and in order to do that, you need to make sure they are with you, focused and engaged.

A funny thing happens when you focus strongly on persuading your audience to transform. You lose all fear, all stage fright, because your focus is no longer on how you feel but on the audience. What's more, because you're so strongly imbued with purpose and passion, you become a compelling, commanding figure. Just the fact that you are standing before the group gives you a head start when it comes to leading them. Clear purpose and command of your presentation will enhance that head start immeasurably.

At this point, if you have done all the things suggested in this book, you will find yourself in command. You'll be in command of your own feelings, your material, the sales process, the showmanship—and your audience. After a few presentations, you'll find that you're having fun when you present, that you have truly taken on the identity of the powerful wizard, able to transform and empower your audiences through your presentations.

Leave Your Audience with a Memorable Conclusion

Just as your presentation needs a clear opening that will set up your audience for what is to follow, it also needs a clear ending. In books and dramatic pieces, we think of the opening as the entrance into the world of the story. The ending returns the readers or audience members to their own world, but with a final message that will help them clearly remember and understand the experience they've been through.

To create a clear ending, I like to think of a tag line that sums up the point and purpose of the talk. At the end of a short story, the tag line might be "And the moral of the story is . . . X." It's worth spending some time to figure out your best possible tag line. It's also a great idea to repeat your name and thank your audience at the end of your talk. Many people have difficulty remembering the names of folks they've just met, and if you're presenting with a purpose, you'll want your audience to remember you and to know how to continue the conversation your presentation has launched.

Here's an example of how I wound up a recent presentation. The slide on the screen was an altered version of the famous Uncle Sam "I Want You" recruiting poster in which the Uncle Sam character is wearing a wizard's pointed hat and using a wand to point directly at the audience. To go with the visual image, I delivered these lines: "I hope you'll all join me on the wizard's path. The world needs more true wizards! I'm Tobias Beckwith. Have a wonderful day, and thank you."

Enjoy the Applause!

If you've given your audience a meaningful presentation, one that has taken them through one or more stimulating stories and inspired them to take action, that audience will want to reward you with their applause. Many first-time presenters—often, those who have trouble connecting with their audience—are uncomfortable when receiving applause. Too many of us have been taught not to do things that will call attention to ourselves and not to show off.

If you're going to become a great presenter, you need to get over the fear of applause, the fear of really connecting, the fear of people looking at you. A true power presenter is a real wizard who takes personal responsibility for the experiences of his or her audience and allows listeners to get the feeling of completion they need at the end of the talk; offering the speaker a healthy round of applause is an important part of the audience's experience. Of course, many presenters love to receive applause, and I expect that you will learn to love it, too. Applause is a form of immediate feedback that lets you know you've done a great job, and it's something to be savored.

All that said, here is a quick piece of advice: Not all audiences feel the need to give applause. If you give a talk and don't get applause at the end, don't let it bother you. In some cultures and situations, applause is thought to be impolite or inappropriate. Therefore, if you get a rousing round of applause one night and nothing the next, don't be too disappointed. Often the non-applauding audience has enjoyed and been moved by your talk just as much as the one that gives a standing ovation.

However a particular audience chooses to express their appreciation, please take the time to give them a bow and to acknowledge their appreciation. You've earned it, and they've earned the right to give it to you, so don't cut them short. You've shared a great experience with this group, and it will be a more satisfying experience for all if you give them the ritual of a formal bow, wave, and your thanks.

Into the Fray!

That's it! You now have the basic knowledge you need to create and deliver a great presentation—except for the most important thing: the experience of actually doing it. Use the information I've given you to structure your talk, build spectacle into it, and then rehearse. All of the preliminaries will be useful, but you will need to make a regular practice of getting in front of audiences and delivering your talks in order to master the art of giving powerful, persuasive presentations. Audiences don't always respond as you expect them to, so it's a good idea to try your new presentation on several small audiences before you take it in front of the one that matters most—whether that audience consists of conference attendees, potential investors, or employees of a business that is an important potential client. Only actually doing the talk in front of those audiences will give you the experience and the confidence you need to shine.

The great news is that if you use what you've learned here and if you get yourself in front of audiences as often as possible, you will quickly develop into a powerful and persuasive presenter. True wizards don't fear failure. Every attempt teaches them new things, and every attempt moves them closer to their goals. Knowing that you can fail, recover, and try again and again until you succeed gives you great power. Soon you'll find yourself with the power to make a bigger difference in the world than you had ever imagined you could. Welcome to the way of the true wizard!

We hope you have enjoyed **The Wizard's Way to Powerful Presentations**. *Please visit http://www.wizardsway.net to learn about the author's other books, presentations and special workshops for presenters. A book can only contain information. You need hands-on experience to master this skill. Tobias Beckwith has helped many top performers in the world of business, but also actors, magicians and others to drastically lift the level of their presentations, all in a very short time via his consultations and workshops. Visit the web site or drop him a line for further information:*

tobias@yourmagic.com

www.ingramcontent.com/pod-product-compliance
Lightning Source LLC
Chambersburg PA
CBHW050954050726
47592CB00007B/2561